296.09   38832

Neusner, Jacob
Torah Through the
Ages.

Torah Through the Ages

TORAH
THROUGH THE AGES

A Short History of Judaism

JACOB NEUSNER

SCM PRESS
London

TRINITY PRESS INTERNATIONAL
Philadelphia

First published 1990

SCM Press Ltd
26–30 Tottenham Road
London N1 4BZ

Trinity Press International
3725 Chestnut Street
Philadelphia, Pa. 19104

© Jacob Neusner 1990

British Library Cataloguing in Publication Data

Neusner, Jacob, *1932–*
    Torah through the ages: a short history of Judaism.
    1. Judaism, History
    I. Title
    296.09

    ISBN 0–334–02456–0
    ISBN 0–334–02440–4 pbk

Library of Congress Cataloging-in-Publication Data

Neusner, Jacob, 1932–
    Torah through the ages: a short history of Judaism/Jacob
    Neusner.
        p.   cm.
    ISBN 0–334–02456–0 — ISBN 0–334–02440–4 (pbk.)
    1. Judaism – History.   2. Rabbinical literature – History and
    criticism.   I. Title.
    BM155.2.N47   1990
    200'00–dc20   89–20645

Phototypeset by Input Typesetting Ltd, London
and printed in Great Britain by
Richard Clay Ltd, Bungay

In memory of my cousin

LOUIS NEUSNER

Whose death deprived all who loved him
of his gifts of love and friendship, lavished on us all
and whose wife and sons, joined by his entire family,
will grieve for him always

Contents

Preface

This short history of Judaism defines the work of seeing together, in brief rehearsal, the entire history of a religion, and then it carries out that work. I explain how we may study as a continuous and unfolding story the history of a religion. Precisely what to do and how to do it, however, requires explanation. Do I promise to tell in brief form everything that ever happened in the name of "Judaism"? Shall I report all the books, holy persons, events and ideas that people anywhere and any time identified as Judaism? Obviously not. Even for so small a religion as Judaism, with only a few million adherents in the world today and fewer in times past, such a single unitary picture would vastly misrepresent as uniformity the facts of diversity and discontinuity. Not only so, but the notion that a religion begins at a given point and has a history from then onward, represents a theological apologetic, not a historical judgment formed on factual grounds.

This book presents a solution to the problem of defining a religion and then composing the history of that religion, thus "a short history . . . " If I succeed in these pages, you should be able to do the same for other religions – Christianity or Islam or Buddhism for instance – replicating my methods and results with appropriate modifications to accommodate the special traits of data of a different order. Further, you should grasp and thus make some sense of the religion, "Judaism" – all together, all at once, and on its own terms. That is my goal. How successfully I attain that goal you must decide at the end of these pages.

Accomplishing the historical task, of course, can serve theology and not the study of religion. The conception that a religion has a history itself forms the expression of the theology of that religion. By appealing to a starting point from which a single continuous history commenced, we assume as matters of fact and description the traits

ix

for that religion of cogency, unity, and order. Then there exists an orthodoxy that is accessible to description, and establishing facts settles questions of faith. By definition, however, points of origin are never accessible to us later on, since what is new germinates over time, and only long after the advent of the new do people acknowledge that something important and unprecedented has happened. Then, long after the fact, facts are chosen, arranged, or invented to account for beginnings, claiming for what has happened the legitimacy that is bestowed by the facts of a singular point of origination.

That the quest for a beginning and the search for the legitimacy of the order attained later on represent a theological act of imagination is now recognized in the study of the history of Christianity. As Burton Mack has stated:

> the scholarly quest for the origins of Christianity has, in effect, been driven by the Christian imagination. Though the gospel story has been critically analyzed at the level of its textual history, at another level, the level of the scholarly imagination of Christian origins, the claims of the gospel have been accepted as self-evident. What if the notion of a single, miraculous point of origin was acknowledged for what it was, not a category of critical scholarship at all, but an article of faith derived from Christian mythology? Then the quest would have to be turned around. Not the mythic events at the beginning, but the social and intellectual occasions of their being imagined would be the thing to understand.[1]

The consequences for the history of Judaism of Mack's reconstituting of the study of the earliest history of Christianity are worked out in the pages of this book.

If theology can define the stakes, in this book I mean to speak about the faith rather than rehearsing the faith or replicating its convictions and paraphrasing its holy writings in secular language. How shall I do this? Here I define what I mean by Judaism, that is, taking account of the diversity of Judaisms over time and space. I do not make the theological judgment that there has been and is now only one Judaism, which would permit me to ignore all other Judaisms. Rather, I specify of which Judaism I speak, and I also justify why I impute to a particular Judaism a continuous and

[1]Burton L. Mack, *A Myth of Innocence. Mark and Christian Origins* (Philadelphia: Fortress Press, 1988), 8–9.

essentially unitary history. This involves an act of selection that is not essentially the imposition of my taste and judgment. Instead, it represents a simple appeal to the prevailing symbolic structure that has characterized all Judaisms and the particular formulation of those symbols that has characterized this Judaism.

I select among the principal symbolic components of any Judaism the symbol of Torah (defined in Chapter 2). That symbol is available in any Judaism, for all Judaisms appeal to the opaque symbols represented, in verbal terms, by the words "God," "Torah," and "Israel." These cyphers stand in secular language for the "world-view," "way of life," and "social entity" that comprise a religion. Every Judaism through time has appealed to the same categories. When the symbols cease to be opaque and become translucent, we may distinguish one Judaism from another. When a given Judaic system speaks of Torah in one way, telling its story in one set of terms rather than in some other, we may differentiate that Judaism from other Judaisms that speak of Torah in some other way and narrate a different myth.

In these pages, then, I appeal to one of the three principal components of the symbolic structure of any Judaism, the symbol of Torah, and in telling its story I claim to narrate in a brief and accessible form the entire history of Judaism: the Judaism of the Torah read in one way rather than in some other, as later chapters will explain. The order of exposition is simple. I start with the largest questions of context and definition. Once I have explained the terms and frame of reference, I proceed systematically to provide a narrative-history of Judaism through the story of what happened in a given Judaism to the symbol of the Torah. That, sum and substance, defines the problem, the proposition, and the argument of this book. Everything beyond this point is meant to spell out the consequences of this approach to composing the short (or long) history of a particular Judaism. Then the difference between short and long is simply the amount of detail to be included to make the main point; readers can readily turn to sustained accounts of every topic in these pages.

My own writings provide occasions for amplification of the topics treated here in the context of a single, unitary, and continuous history of Judaism. In other writings I have set forth a field-theory for the entire history of Judaism: beginnings, middle, and present. I have, furthermore, set forth the religion, history, and literature of Judaism in its formative age and in contemporary times in a variety of writings. These books contribute to the conceptions and formulations of this short history of Judaism, although this book not only stands on its own but also sets forth an essentially fresh representation of matters. The prior writings on which I have drawn for ideas and occasionally for verbatim expression of ideas are as follows:

1. Field-theory
Self-Fulfilling Prophecy: Exile and Return in the History of Judaism. Boston: Beacon Press, 1987.

2. Beginnings
Judaism and Christianity in the Age of Constantine: Issues in the Initial Confrontation. Chicago: The University of Chicago Press, 1987.
Judaism in the Beginning of Christianity. Philadelphia: Fortress Press, 1983; British edition, London: SPCK, 1984.
Judaism in the Matrix of Christianity. Philadelphia: Fortress Press, 1986.

3. To the present day
Death and Birth of Judaism: The Impact of Christianity, Secularism, and the Holocaust on Jewish Faith. New York: Basic Books, 1987.

4. Religion, history, and literature of Judaism in its formative age and afterward
The Enchantments of Judaism. Rites of Transformation from Birth through Death. New York: Basic Books, 1988.
Way of Torah: An Introduction to Judaism. Fourth edition, completely revised. Belmont: Wadsworth, 1988.
The Foundations of Judaism. Philadelphia: Fortress Press, 1989.
Invitation to Midrash: The Working of Rabbinic Bible Interpretation. San Francisco: Harper & Row, 1988.
What is Midrash? Philadelphia: Fortress Press, 1987.
Invitation to the Talmud. San Francisco: Harper & Row, 1984.
Judaism. The Evidence of the Mishnah. Chicago: University of Chicago Press, 1981; second edition, augmented: Atlanta: Scholars Press, 1987 (Brown Judaic Studies).
Judaism in Society: The Evidence of the Yerushalmi. Toward the Natural History of a Religion. Chicago: University of Chicago Press, 1983.
Judaism and Scripture: The Evidence of Leviticus Rabbah. Chicago: University of Chicago Press, 1986.

Judaism: The Classical Statement. The Evidence of the Bavli. Chicago:
   University of Chicago Press, 1986.
Judaism and Story: The Evidence of The Fathers According to Rabbi Nathan.
   Chicago: University of Chicago Press, 1990.
*Vanquished Nation, Broken Spirit. The Virtues of the Heart in Formative
   Judaism.* New York: Cambridge University Press, 1987.
Judaism and its Social Metaphors. Israel in the History of Jewish Thought.
   Cambridge and New York: Cambridge University Press, 1988.
The Incarnation of God: The Character of Divinity in Formative Judaism.
   Philadelphia: Fortress Press, 1988.
*Writing with Scripture: The Authority and Uses of the Hebrew Bible in the
   Torah of Formative Judaism.* Philadelphia: Fortress Press, 1989.
Between Time and Eternity. The Essentials of Judaism. Encino: Dickenson
   Publishing Co, 1976. Fifth printing, Belmont: Wadsworth, 1983.
Stranger at Home. Zionism, "The Holocaust," and American Judaism.
   Chicago: University of Chicago Press, 1980.
From Testament to Torah: An Introduction to Judaism in its Formative Age.
   Englewood Cliffs: Prentice Hall, 1987.

In addition, my chapter on "Judaism" in *World Religions* (San
Francisco: Harper & Row, 1992, edited by Arvin Sharma) has
contributed formulations here and there. Each of the above titles
expands on subjects treated briefly here. All of these books make
their own points, but I also revise and reshape matters stated in
other contexts as I develop my proposition and argument in this
book. What I propose in these pages draws upon completed work
and reshapes it all in the service of solving the single problem
addressed here.

As this book was getting under way, my cousin, Louis Neusner,
died suddenly. He was a sweet and loving person, whom all of us
privileged to be in his generation of the Neusner family cherished
and loved. All of us are bereaved by his sudden death at a relatively
early age. We wanted him as the solace of our old age, but we bury
him in the prime of his life. The dedication of this book is my
memorial to someone of whom I was very fond and in whom I took
great pride. My heart goes out to his wife and two sons, who bear for
us all the burden of this grievous tragedy.

                                             JACOB NEUSNER

*Institute for Advanced Study, Princeton,
New Jersey*

Prologue

If by "Judaism" we mean anything any Jews anywhere have ever believed about God, their society, and the meaning of life, then there is not now and there never has been a single Judaism. Taken all together, Jews have believed everything and its opposite about the critical components of a religion: God, community, and the holy way of life. It follows, therefore, that no one can write a history of Judaism, short or long. It is the simple fact that the history of Judaism that is continuous, unitary, and uniform never took place and cannot be told. In any single era there has been, as today there is, diversity and, over time, there has been only change. So whence *the* Judaism that will have its continuous and harmonious history written? As one recent book (that nevertheless purports to write *the* history of Judaism) says explicitly, "Judaism has been and continues to be a dynamic and pluralistic religion with a common core of faith that has changed and adapted to the time, spirit, and conditions of the varying cultures and ages it has encountered."[1] Clearly a "common core of faith" that changes and adapts over time loses whatever "core" it had to begin with.

Anyone who imagines that "faith" in a propositional sense (expressed in words about God, revelation, the character of the social entity that is holy, and the like) can remain the same over thousands of years in a vast range of languages and cultures, must tell us precisely how words can ever remain so stable and uniform as to say the same thing in so many different ways – and how we are to find out what that one thing is. Only a theological formulation, not a descriptive and factual one, can sustain such a conviction. But

---

[1] Phillip Sigal, *Judaism: The Evolution of a Faith*. Revised and edited by Lillian Sigal (Grand Rapids: Eerdmans, 1989), 1. Cited further on are other passages in this same book.

1

theology in historical form, while commonplace, deceives. For it does not deliver what it promises, and it distorts what it purports to provide. It is bad history and bad theology: bad history because it is fabricated; bad theology because it is unarticulated.

I do not mean to suggest that people who recognize changes over time and space and over long stretches of human experience draw the correct conclusion, that is, that there is no single Judaism, and therefore there can be no continuous and harmonious history of Judaism (or, I should imagine, any other religion of dimensions and endurance). Rather, they may announce that there is no continuity, but then they proceed to tell the story of a continuous and unfolding religion by picking and choosing in any given age what sustained Judaism for that moment and, more importantly, omitting reference to what did not. In this manner the historian settles the claim of normativity and religious truth. But the act of choice in the guise of mere description represents a theological judgment, not a historical one. The most current example of how people recognize and then deny the diversities that require us to speak only of Judaisms admits "the continuity of the entire historical process." Then, talking of change and adaptation, the same writer proceeds to narrate a single, continuous tale of one unitary Judaism over time.

In the example at hand, which is representative of an entire genre of writing histories of the Jews or of Judaism, the author treats "proto-Judaism" (ca. 2000–400 BCE), surveying in sequence (as though the biblical narrative were an account of historical events in order) the time of the patriarchs, Moses, judges, monarchy; Judaism after the Babylonian exile (400 BCE–70 CE), Rabbinic Judaism, the medieval era, philosophy and mysticism; proto-modernity (the influence of the Renaissance on Judaism, the Protestant Reformation and Judaism); the modern and contemporary periods (Reform, traditionalist opposition to Reform, Neo-Orthodoxy; Hasidism, Judaism in North America; Zionism, the Holocaust, and the State of Israel), then Judaism distilled: doctrines, ethics, ritual. All of these things, however, do not add up to one thing; they remain many, diverse, and incoherent.

Furthermore these categories are not really similar or alike. Some of these subjects are not religious but political (Zionism, for instance); some of them are ethnic and secular (the Holocaust); and some of them do not even focus upon Judaism at all (the influence of the

Renaissance, an odd choice indeed, since most Jews lived where the Renaissance never reached). The repertoire of topics is wildly incoherent because the categories are unlike one another in their very form. In fact, in their basic convictions, they contradict one another. So the representation of a single, linear, harmonious Judaism from 2000 BCE[!] to the present is in no sense historical.

As a next logical step we must ask: Then what of the histories of the Jews? If, as I have suggested, there is no one Judaism, then surely there must be a single Jewish people, and one can certainly write a history of that people, if not of its religion. The subject, "Jewish history," however, is as difficult to justify as "the history of Judaism." The conception that there is a single, unitary, and continuous history of the Jews is a commonplace, but each time someone attempts to tell that story, the same process of normative selection gets underway. Paul Johnson's *History of the Jews*[2] is a striking example of the difficulty of making sense of a single, unitary history of the Jews. The author perceives the Jews as having a "separate and specific identity earlier than almost any other people which still survives," and he thus believes that the Jews have a separate and single specific identity which they have maintained. He does not explain what he means by "identity." At the center of his book, however, is the premise that a single group, which everywhere and at all times exhibited the same indicative traits, formed a single unitary and linear history with a beginning, middle, and, so far, a happy end.

The composition of such a continuous, unitary history of the Jews, like the formation of a single history of Judaism, constitutes a theological act. For speaking descriptively, we cannot identify such a single group with fixed and ubiquitously uniform traits. To Johnson everything Jewish relates to everything else Jewish, with slight regard to circumstance and context. Johnson's notion of a single, linear "Jewish history," which he can tell as story, expresses not theology but ideology. His story is one of blood and peoplehood that represents a single group where there have been many, and he works out a single linear history where there has been none.

For most of their history prior to 586 BCE Jews lived in various countries. Each country and its Jews worked out their own localized

---

[2] Paul Johnson, *A History of the Jews* (London: Weidenfeld and Nicolson, 1988 and San Francisco: Harper & Row, 1987).

history, whether in the Land of Israel ("Palestine") or Babylonia, whether in Morocco or Spain, Iraq or Tunisia, or France or the USA. The histories of such diverse groups of Jews cannot be linked together into a single linear and unitary history, that is, into a story that we can tell in a simple sequence: first came France, then the USA. Each history, whether Babylonian from 586 BCE to 1949 or American from 1964 to the present, holds together on its own terms and tells its own distinct and distinctive story. Sewing these histories together into a continuous story yields "first they went here, then they went there," an itinerary followed by only a few.

Histories of Judaism and histories of the Jews that pick and choose and do not say so represent the intellectual version of a theology and an ideology. The theology is an essentially secular-ethnic one, and the ideology is Zionist-nationalist. These joined constructions answer critical and important questions for Jews regarding whence they have come and where they are heading and what their life together means. The neat picture painted by a single, linear, and unitary history conveys a message of proportion, sense, and order. But alas, such a one-level history selects a little and leaves out a lot. There is not now nor has there ever been a single Judaism. Nevertheless one Judaism has predominated for a long time. There is not now nor has there ever been a single "Jewish identity" which Jews have uniformly preserved unchanged from some mythic beginning to this morning. One history covering all Jews, beginning to the present, has never existed. But a single ideology does indeed demand the rehearsal of a single history and, in the service of contemporary ethnic celebration, such a history performs well.

That will not be so in the pages of this book. Here, for merely descriptive reasons, I have identified a single Judaism or Judaic system among many, and I tell the history of that Judaism which, I claim, exhibits definitive traits of continuity, harmony, cogency, and uniformity. It is a Judaism that puts forth an enduring symbolic structure, that absorbs within that structure all manner of accretions, changing and accommodating what is new to conform to its enduring system, drawing strength from what fits, gaining vigor through rejecting what does not. This book rests upon the claim, specifically, that a single symbol does remain constant, that what happens to that symbol over time proves coherent, and that we can establish criteria for inclusion and also exclusion. By appeal to the symbol of Torah as one Judaism defined that symbol and referred to it, we can tell *the history of the Judaism of the Torah*, which is, in fact, the Judaism that has predominated from the age in which it took shape to our own day – and which gives every evidence of flourishing into the century that will commence shortly.

1

Torah through the Ages

Since different groups of Jews have, over time, framed for themselves diverse Judaisms, each with its generative symbol, world-view, way of life, and definition of themselves as "Israel," one wonders how there can be a single, unitary, harmonious, and continuous history of Judaism or of the Jews. As I have explained, the simple answer is that there cannot be such a history. But there can be, in brief sketch, the history of the Judaism that proved normative over time and that today defines the terms for all other Judaic systems. And that Judaism does have a continuous, linear, and unitary history because, by appeal to its critical symbols, we may account for all developments that took place within its framework, and we may also exclude from consideration all Judaisms that did not. When we do, we find ourselves tracing a continuous path from the point of origin to the present day.

This Judaism may be delineated in a simple and clear way, in a definition that includes only this Judaism and excludes all others. It is the one and only one that appealed for its generative symbol to "the Torah," meaning God's revelation to Moses at Sinai. Other Judaisms appealed to the Mosaic legislation (submission to the authority of the Torah of Moses at Sinai marks all Judaisms as Judaic and excludes all other religions as not-Judaic). But this is the one that claimed a particular form and tradition to have originated at Sinai, a version of Moses's Torah that no other Judaism accepted. Furthermore, it is the sole Judaism that defined its way of life so as to sanctify the here and now, and that framed its world-view around salvation at the end of time with the coming of the Messiah.

Among all Judaisms, moreover, it is unique in its catholic definition

6

of "Israel," that is, the social entity that realized in the here and now the world-view and way of life of the system. Other Judaisms, the Essene Judaism of the Dead Sea Scrolls, for example, proved exclusive and defined as "Israel" only a very few persons, that is, its own adherents. But the Judaism we are delineating defined "Israel" in the broadest possible way to encompass all Jews bearing genealogical ties, through the mother, to the family of Abraham, Isaac, and Jacob and, paradoxically, all persons who accepted the Torah and its disciplines from late antiquity to our own day. It excluded not sinners but only those who denied the most fundamental principles of the world-view, for instance, that the belief in the resurrection of the dead (which many Judaisms affirmed) derived from the Torah.

This definition of "Israel" in the following surely means to extend to their outermost limits the boundaries of "Israel":

A. All Israelites have a share in the world to come,

B. as it is said, "Your people also shall be all righteous, they shall inherit the land forever; the branch of my planting, the work of my hands, that I may be glorified" (Is. 60:21).

C. And these are the ones who have no portion in the world to come: (1) He who says that the resurrection of the dead is a teaching which does not derive from the Torah, (2) or that the Torah does not come from Heaven; or (3) an Epicurean.

Mishnah-Tractate Sanhedrin 10:1

In context the exclusions prove few and the inclusions prove many. Moreover, this formulation of matters proves emblematic for the range of concern of the Judaism at hand: inclusive, welcoming, vastly proselytizing within the ethnic group in behalf of its particular reading of the life of the group.

True, there were other Judaisms before, and there have been and now are other Judaisms in modern times, each of which has framed its symbolic system and ordered its social entity without perpetual appeal to the Torah – Zionism and the Judaism of Holocaust and Redemption, to take two modern instances; or the Essene Judaism known from the Dead Sea Scrolls, to take an ancient one. From the point at which the Judaism that focused upon the Torah took the field, however, all known heresies defined themselves against it, and all other Judaisms took shape in relationship to it. That is a mark of

its paramount and definitive status, hence its normative character
in its time.

When there was a heresy, it identified as its critical issue a primary
concern of this Judaism, and rejected that doctrine. One important
example: In early medieval times in the Islamic world, a Judaism
took shape called Karaism. Its principal position was that the
writings that the normative Judaism called "the oral Torah" were
not divine in their origin and did not go back all the way to Sinai in
a chain of tradition through oral formulation and oral transmission.
Only the written Torah, what we know as the Pentateuch or the
Five Books of Moses, carried God's authority. Karaism therefore
represents a heresy defined in terms of and over against the Judaism
that predominated.

When there was a major new development as, for instance, the
formation of a rich mystical life, the framers and founders identified
their ideas with the Torah of the Judaism that was normative.
Accordingly, the authorities of the Torah contributed their names
as authors of writings much later on, or as authorities in those
writings, so that the new and unprecedented system of thought and
piety legitimated itself by appeal to the established Judaism. The
Zohar, a great work of mystical theology and piety, claimed to tell
the story of Simeon b. Yohai and other ancient rabbis and thus found
a place for the new doctrines in the old Torah. As such, the
Zohar represents a new development that defined itself within
the established symbolic structure of the established Judaism. By
contrast, in the nineteenth and twentieth century, Judaisms took
shape that did not appeal to the symbols and social order defined by
the Torah at hand – Zionism, as one example; the Judaism of
Holocaust and Redemption (matching the destruction of European
Jewry from 1933 to 1945 with the formation of the State of Israel in
1948), as another.

When a Judaism has the power to dictate the terms of both its
opposition (heresies) and its innovation, extension, and expansion,
it occupies the center and defines the norm. From late antiquity to
the present, there has been and is now only one such Judaism. In
terms of religion, it is today the only religious formulation of a Jewish
system – world-view, way of life, definition of the social entity,
"Israel" – that circulates. There are secular Jewish systems that
compete – Zionism (the doctrine that Jews form a political entity

and should have a state) and Israelism (centering of Jewish life in the State of Israel and its affairs), as one example; ways of life and world-views that center upon culture or politics, as another. As far as a group of Jews understand themselves in terms that people in general classify as religious – appeal to God, revelation, categories of sanctification and salvation – the only Judaism (in numerous variations to be sure) is the one that speaks about the Torah and reads as canonical the holy books identified with the Judaism of the Torah.

In what follows, I present a brief account of the major chapters in the unfolding of this Judaism. But what sort of picture of the life of a sector of humanity emerges, and what can we expect to learn about the potentialities of the human race from this story of Torah through the ages? To understand the choices, let me compare the shape and structure of a short history of Christianity with the counterpart of Judaism.

A short history of Christianity encompasses the history of Western civilization. Captured in the central symbol of Jesus, the unfolding of the structure and dynamic of the life of the West may be portrayed by what people said about and how they represented him.[1] A short history of Judaism by contrast tells a different story. The Jews did not define the civilization of the West, they responded to it. Captured in the central symbol of the Torah, which stands for what God wants from Israel (the holy people who lived by the Torah), the story of loyalty, endurance, and courage may be told. True, it is not the tale of the building of the world civilization that the West has made. Rather, it is the story of how people, through their response to the symbol of the Torah, found the resources to build lives of worth, dignity, and loyalty to God, come what may. So while the history of Judaism tells the story of the underside of Western civilization, from that history too we learn about what was happening to humanity. The difference is that Christianity expressed the sensibility of the rules; Judaism, of the subordinated. Christianity expressed the sensibility of the masters; Judaism, of the survivors.

That lesson, however, has even broader relevance. In an age in which to survive is to have achieved the unexpected, and in a century

---

[1] Jaroslav Pelikan accomplishes this in his brilliant *Jesus Through the Centuries* (New Haven: Yale University Press, 1985).

in which the collapse of civilization brought about the death through war of hundreds of millions of human beings, we would do well to see how survivors endure. For Israel, the Jewish people, the record of enduring in hope, making do in patience, and affirming in courage also forms the heritage of the West where, after all, there have always been more ruled than rulers and more victims on the cross (even entire nations in Africa, Asia, Latin America, and Europe itself). Perhaps the age beyond our own will find opportunity to renew the civilization that Christianity made in the West. Then, in that new age of rebuilding, the record of the great vision of a world in the service of God will encompass even those who, like Israel in the West, served and now serve by enduring.

The odd couple, those who *did* and those who *endured*, join not by accident but by each party's understanding of the divine intent. Both Judaism and Christianity claim to be the heirs and products of the Hebrew Scriptures: Tanakh to the Jews, Old Testament to the Christians.[2] So the story of the West encompasses both legacies – the Christian vision of the society and civilization to realize the teachings of Jesus and the Judaic vision of the society and civilization of the Torah. These form counterparts that can stand comparison with one another. That is why a knowledge of Torah through the ages may stand alongside a knowledge of Jesus through the ages. To be sure, what we know is different in each case. But in the Scriptures that are shared, each bears part of the undivided heritage of Scripture which speaks to rulers and ruled, those who do and those who endure.

What form would Western civilization have taken had the Judaic rather than the Christian formulation of the heritage of Hebrew Scriptures come to predominate? What sort of society would have emerged? How would people have regulated their affairs? What would have been the shape of the prevailing value systems? Behind the immense varieties of Christian life and Christian and post-

---

[2] True, both great religious traditions derive not solely or directly from the authority and teachings of these Scriptures, but rather from the ways in which that authority has been mediated and those teachings interpreted through other holy books. The New Testament is the prism through which the light of the Old comes to Christianity. The canon of rabbinical writings is the star that guides Jews to the revelation of Sinai, the Torah. But the Hebrew Scriptures produced the two interrelated, yet quite separate groups of religious societies that formed Judaism and Christianity.

Christian society stand the evocative teachings and theological and moral convictions assigned by Christian belief to the figure of Christ. To be a Christian in some measure meant and means to seek to be like him in one of the many ways in which Christians envisage him.

To be a Jew may similarly be reduced to the single, pervasive symbol of Judaism: Torah. To be a Jew meant to live the life of Torah in one of the many ways in which the masters of Torah taught. We know what the figure of Christ has meant to the art, music, and literature of the West; the church to its politics, history, and piety; Christian faith to its values and ideals. It is much more difficult to say what Torah would have meant to creative arts, the course of relations among nations and people, and the hopes and aspirations of ordinary folk. Between Christ, universally known and triumphant, and Torah, the spiritual treasure of a tiny, harassed, abused people, seldom fully known and never long victorious, stands the abyss: mastery of the world on the one side and the sacrifice of the world on the other.

Perhaps the difference comes at the very start when the Christians, despite horrendous suffering, determined to conquer and save the world and to create the new Israel. The rabbis, unmolested and unimpeded, set forth to transform and regenerate the old Israel. For the former, the arena of salvation was all humankind and the actor was a single man. For the latter, the course of salvation began with Israel, God's first love, and the stage was that singular but paradigmatic society, the Jewish people. It was the Torah that defined the life of that people so that, come what may, Israel, the people, always and everywhere found life worth living.

Let me conclude with some specific definitions of the categories I propose to use. Dealing with the problem of the diversity of Judaisms within Judaism proves somewhat easier if instead of "religion" we speak of "religious system." A religious system comprises three components:

1. A world-view, explaining who people are, where they come from, what they must do; in general, what a Judaism defines as "the Torah" will contain that world-view;

2. A way of life, expressing in concrete deeds that world-view and linking the life of the individual to polity; what a Judaism sets forth as the things someone must do as, for instance, "halakhah" in the Judaism of the dual Torah, describes that holy way of life;

3. A particular social group, in the case of a Judaic system, an "Israel," to whom the world-view and way of life refer; all Judaisms define that social group by saying who and what is "Israel."

A Judaic system, a Judaism, comprises a world-view, a way of life, and a group of Jews who hold the one and live by the other. When we speak of a Judaism, therefore, we point to a given world-view, way of life, and social group that have coalesced in a definitive way. How do we discern that occasion of coalescence? We look for appeal to a striking and distinctive symbol, something that expresses the whole all together and all at once. For the symbol – whether visual or verbal, whether in gesture or in song or in dance, or whether even in the definition of the role of woman – will capture the whole and proclaim its special message: its way of life, its world-view, its definition of who is Israel. In the case of a Judaism, such a generative symbol may derive from the word "Torah," meaning God's revelation to Moses at Sinai. Or it may come to concrete form in the word "Israel," meaning God's holy people. Or, of course, the generative symbol may come to concrete expression in the conception of God. All Judaisms define God, Torah, and Israel. If we trace the way in which a Judaic system works out its conceptions of these over time, we can indeed follow the history of that Judaism. While it is a fact that through the history of the Jewish people, diverse Judaisms have won the allegiance of groups of Jews here and there, each system did specify the things it regarded as urgent both in belief and in behavior. While all systems in common allege that they represent the true and authentic Judaism or Torah or will of God for Israel, and that their devotees *are* Israel, none has succeeded in persuading any other of its views. All have in common the appeal to opaque symbols. Once defined by one, the symbol becomes useless to the others.

This explains how important it is for a Judaism not only to say it is the only Judaism, but also to trace for itself a history from beginning to present, a history that is exclusive and exclusionary. For the conception of a single, unitary, harmonious history, from a distinct point of origin to the present, forms a principal part of the world-view of any Judaism. Each Judaism ordinarily situates itself along a single historical line (hence a linear history) from the entirety of the past. A Judaism ordinarily sees itself as the natural outgrowth or increment of time and change. These traits of historical or even supernatural origin characterize nearly all Judaisms. How then do we know one from another? When we can identify the principal symbol to which a given system on its own appeals, we realize that we have a wholly distinct and distinctive system in prospect.

These, then, are the terms that define the categories of inquiry in this book. Now that we know what we learn about religion from studying Judaism in particular, let us start from the beginning. That means we must begin with Judaism in the world today, what most people know from the everyday world of neighbors on the one side and headlines in the newspapers on the other.

2

Defining a Judaism

Judaism encompasses a variety of closely related religious systems, past and present. These systems share a number of traits. For example, all of them revere the Torah revealed by God to Moses at Sinai. That is what justifies classifying all of them as Judaisms. But they also differ among themselves in important ways. To define Judaism as a unitary and uniform religion, unfolding in a single continuous history from beginning to present, therefore, is simply not possible. The world today knows a number of Judaisms, and times past witnessed diversity as well. To use a familiar example: if you know Reform Jews, you realize that some biblical laws about food do not enjoy prominence in their Judaism; if you know Orthodox Jews, you recognize that they keep the Sabbath as a holy day.

In these concrete ways the patterns of religious observance and belief that characterize Reform Jews and those that mark Orthodox Jews bear little in common. How can God want me not to eat pork and not to perform mundane labor on the Sabbath, as Orthodox Judaism maintains on the strength of Scripture and at the same time not care what I do at the table and on specified holy days, as Reform Judaism maintains, appealing to the same Scripture (if in different aspects)? Instead of trying to harmonize clearly distinct Judaisms, whether two thousand years ago or today, we would do better to recognize difference and deal with it. Much of our study of Judaism will address this very problem. When we face this problem in Judaism, we shall learn how to deal with diversity within other religions as well.

A second reason that Judaism is difficult to define will strike you as equally obvious: while some Jews are Reform or Orthodox,

Conservative or Reconstructionist, other Jews are not at all religious in any sense you can understand. You realize, then, that there are Jews who are secular. Since people generally assume that "Judaism is the religion of the Jewish people," they identify the ethnic group with the religion. That makes it difficult to define Judaism for a simple reason: not all Jews are religious in any sense at all. Even more important, many Jews are religious in ways that Christians do not recognize as religious, and are not religious in ways that Christians take for granted religiosity requires.

For example, Christianity does not regard obeying dietary laws as religious. Yet there are secular Jews who do not eat pork, and avoiding forbidden foods in Judaism is religious, not merely ethnic. Christianity in its Protestant forms regards personal prayer as critical in the religious life. But, like other religious, many Judaisms place heavier emphasis on the recitation of prescribed liturgy and less on the personal intentionality that is supposed to accompany prayer. When we study Judaism, we find ourselves redefining what we mean by religion. In so far as all religions can be distinguished in affirming the existence of God, and all modes of secularity are characterized by atheism, there are, in fact, Jews who in no way are religious. That calls into question the ethnic definition of Judaism as "the religion of the Jewish people."

Many of the Jews you know are apt to strike you as less engaged by the synagogue than their counterparts in Christianity and Islam are by the church and the mosque. You therefore wonder whether Judaism is a religion at all. But what makes you doubt that Judaism falls into the same class as Christianity and Islam confuses what should be kept distinct. The ethnic group, the Jews, and the religion, Judaism, must be distinguished. The ethnic group, the Jews, encompasses everybody who is rightly regarded as Jewish. On the other hand, not everybody in that ethnic group believes in or practices a Judaism. People think that Jews' views add up to Judaism. That is not so, since Judaism is a religion, and not all Jews are religious. We must therefore distinguish the ethnic group, the Jews or Jewish people, from the religious group that is encompassed by the ethnic group, that is, the Judaists, practitioners of Judaism, who also happen to be Jews. Then we may fairly say that what some Judaists believe does add up to a Judaism, and that permits us to define a particular Judaism. The interplay of the ethnic and the religious is

one of the interesting characteristics of the study of religion that
Judaism makes possible, perhaps more than other religions.

To state the problem simply: if you convert to the Roman Catholic
religion, you do not automatically become Spanish, Italian, or
Brazilian. If you become Episcopalian, you do not automatically get
a British passport or accent. If you convert to Judaism, however, you
automatically become a Jew, a member of the ethnic group. To put
matters differently, no one ever called the Methodists "a people,"
and there is no Presbyterian state. But the Jews are called a people,
there is a Jewish state, and the people and state identify Judaism as
their own religion. What makes Judaism particularly interesting,
therefore, is the opportunity for the study of the relationship of the
ethnic and the religious that it affords.

It follows that once we separate the two and realize that not all
Jews are Judaists or practitioners of Judaism, the confusion between
the opinions held by persons who call themselves Jews and the
religion Judaism is readily sorted out. Since the problem of studying
Judaism in the setting of the study of religion is complicated by that
confusion, let us dwell on the steps just now taken.

1. Judaism is a religion (or, as we already recognize, a set of
religions) and the Jews are an ethnic group;

2. If a person is a Judaist or a practitioner of Judaism, he or she
also is automatically a member of the ethnic group, the Jews;

3. For a long time, through nearly the whole of recorded history,
everyone who was a Jew also was a Judaist.

The upshot is simple. Even if we were to learn "what the Jews
believe," for example, their opinions obtained through public opinion
polling about various questions (whether religious or political or
cultural), we still do not know anything about Judaism. If we can
find out what the Judaists among the Jews believe, we will know
something. What makes matters complicated, of course, is that the
distinction between the ethnic and the religious among people who
are both is not so readily drawn. However, we can at least avoid
some obvious errors by identifying up front the sources of possible
confusion.

In so stating matters, of course, I have moved beyond the limits
of the faith. For every Judaism sees itself as an incremental development, the final and logical outcome of *the* History of Judaism. As we
noted in the Preface, it is in the nature of theology to take precisely

that position. From the perspective of the theologian and the believer, I can imagine no other. Every Judaism commences in the definition of its canon, whether of relevant historical facts or of holy books. All Judaisms therefore testify to humanity's power of creative genius: making something out of nothing. Each creates and defines itself. Every Judaism in modern times alleges that it is the natural or historical Judaism, but that allegation always denies the obvious fact. Each Judaism begins in its own time and place and then goes in search of a useful past. Every system serves to suit a purpose, to solve a problem, to answer through a self-evidently right doctrine a question that none can escape or ignore. Orthodoxy no less than Reform takes up fresh positions and presents stunningly original and relevant innovations.

The reason why a given religion encompasses diverse subdivisions, Judaism encompassing Judaisms, is that religions do not exist in the abstract, in books and in doctrines. Religions flourish in the concrete social world of people solving problems together. Moreover, it is the nature of humanity to divide, like amoebas, and to subdivide. If religion shapes the world, and if a religion is diverse and encompasses a variety of subdivisions, the reason is that religions take up urgent questions and answer them in a manner that believers find self-evidently valid. Since different groups of people identify as urgent their own distinctive questions, it is quite natural that within a large group, adhering to what it conceives to be a single religion, various social entities divided by space, time, and circumstance will shape matters, each in response to its human situation.

Simply stated, a religion shapes the world of its believers by identifying the questions that must find answers and by providing answers that people know to be true. In the nature of things, those who find the answers to be true beyond the need for any argument or discussion form a social entity and define the world of that entity within the limits set by the compelling questions and the persuasive answers of the faith. When we know what questions a religion asks and answers and can say who deems those questions the ones that must be answered, we can define a religion.

The distinction that I have made between the ethnic and the religious works better in theory than in fact. That explains why I have chosen "Torah" for this probe of the history of a given Judaism rather than "Israel."[1] While Judaism imputes much importance to "Israel," meaning "the holy people of God," the ethnic group, that is, the Jewish people, for its part assigns the highest value to Judaism. Consequently, nowadays a person born of a Jewish mother who is an atheist is regarded as a Jew. But a person born of a Jewish mother who accepts a religion other than Judaism is not so regarded. If a person leaves Judaism for another religion, such as Christianity or Islam, that person is generally regarded to have lost a place in the ethnic group; on the other hand, if a person does not believe in or practice (any) Judaism, he or she remains very much part of the ethnic group. The confusion is illustrated by contemporary debates, familiar from one year to the next in the headlines of the newspapers, about "who is a Jew?"

The reason that the issue is not only chronic but sometimes urgent is the confusion of religion and ethnic identification (in the diaspora), or religion and nationality (in the State of Israel). The Israeli parliament, the Knesset, in defining who may become an Israeli citizen, declared in the "law of return" at the foundation of the State of Israel soon after 1948 that any Jew in the world may become an Israeli citizen for the asking. The qualification for citizenship was simply belonging to the ethnic group. But who is in the ethnic group? That issue is not so simple. A convert to Judaism becomes not only a Judaist but a Jew. Then who is a valid convert?

The full complexity of the interplay of the ethnic and the religions in all Judaisms comes to the fore in Israeli politics even now. To make their views part of state law, the Orthodox Judaisms of the State of Israel, organized in political parties and well-represented in the Knesset, have repeatedly asked the government to declare as a Jew by conversion only someone converted "in accord with the law," meaning the law of Judaism. In fact, what the Orthodox Judaic

---

[1] In my *Judaism and its Social Metaphors: Israel in the History of Judaism* (Cambridge and New York: Cambridge University Press, 1989), I have set forth part of the history of "Israel" of the Judaism of the dual Torah among several Judaisms of late antiquity. The same work, of course, is to be done with the opaque symbol of God. I have made a beginning of it in my *The Incarnation of God in Formative Judaism* (Philadelphia: Fortress Press, 1989), but there is much more to be done. I am certain the results will prove congruent for the history of the Judaism of the dual Torah with the results set forth here on the history of that Judaism explored through the symbol of Torah.

leadership means is, "in accord with the law of Judaism as we interpret and apply it," and they explicitly say that only a convert to Orthodox Judaism is a Jew. Converts to Judaism in the Reform or Conservative or Reconstructionist formulations, who in the USA are accepted as full members of the Jewish people and of course as Judaists, are not validly converted. What this has meant is that membership in the ethnic group is defined by religious criteria. We see, therefore, that our theoretical distinction between the ethnic and the religious does not work in practice because the ethnic life of the Jewish people is deeply shaped by the theological convictions of Israel, the holy people of God in Judaism.

In the political crisis of the State of Israel regarding "who is a Jew," we see an intensity of engagement with religion in its most religious formulation: who is holy and who is not. The reason is that "who is a Jew" defines "who is Israel," meaning not state or ethnic group but holy people, that is, a religious category. When Jews debate the profound issues of Jewish existence and Judaic theology, that is the category of which they speak: "Israel." When they debate the definition of "Israel," meaning the Jewish people, they address questions of authenticity and legitimacy that in Christianity form issues of orthodoxy or heresy. The contemporary debates in Jerusalem, harsh and fresh though they appear, in fact continue age-old and important arguments.

From the formation of the Pentateuch in the aftermath of the return to Zion in 586 BCE, people within the Jewish world have, through debates on "who is a Jew," proposed to say who is in and who is out, who is Israel and who is other. Whether it is reflection on the heritage of Abraham, Isaac, and Jacob in the Five Books of Moses formed by Ezra in 450 BCE, or the doctrine of the saving remnant that constitutes "Israel" in the imagination of the Essene community at Qumran, or the apostle St Paul's troubled assessment of the old Israel and the new, or the Talmudic rabbis' insistence on the sanctity and the sanctification of all Israel, the subject "who is Israel" remains one and the same.

The very name of the Jewish state – the State of Israel – tells the story of the union of the ethnic and this-worldly with the religious and the theological. David Ben Gurion's profound understanding led him to name the new state, formed in the Land of Israel by the people of Israel in 1948, "the State of Israel." That is why the

relationship between Zionism and Judaism forms the centerpiece of
contemporary Judaic theology as well as Jewish thought today. In
debating issues as now formulated, with the Israeli legislature passing
laws on "who is a Jew" and with issues of definition of peoplehood,
state, land, and exile forming the center of public discourse, Jews
carry forward in a perfectly straight line the exquisitely theological
discussions that have characterized their shared existence from
remote beginnings. For, as we now realize, every Judaism defines
not only "Judaism" but also "Israel," that is, the social entity that
embodies that Judaism and forms the holy people envisioned within
the given Judaic system. Accordingly, in calling the state simply
"Israel," people deliver a profound statement regarding who (in *their*
opinion, that is, within *their* Judaism) is Israel, what is Israel (a state,
not merely a community; a political entity, not merely a religious
fellowship), who is the true Israel, and similar, long-vexed dilemmas
of religious thinkers in Judaism, past and present, as well as secular
Jewish thinkers today.

Among the many definitions of who is Israel and who is a Jew,
that of the Talmudic rabbis (all Israel, born of a Jewish mother, is
Israel) remains authentic to the liturgy of Judaism, on the one side,
and its Sacred Scripture, on the other. Ben Gurion's daring utilization
of "Israel" in an exclusive and land-centered framework challenges
that liturgy and Scripture. For at prayer and study, "Israel" stands
for the entire Jewish people wherever they live: "God who keeps
Israel does not slumber or sleep" is everywhere and watches over
Israel everywhere, including Israel in the Land of Israel. This brings
us back to the particular Judaism whose history is set forth here –
the Judaism of the dual Torah. To begin with, I offer a clear definition
of that particular Judaism. I choose it simply because it is the
Judaism that predominated from ancient times to our own day.

The Judaism of the dual Torah is the only Judaism ever and
anywhere that appeals to the myth of divine revelation to Moses at
Sinai in two media, oral and written, hence "dual Torah." God gave
the Torah in writing, and that is the Scriptures ("the Old Testament"
of Christianity), in particular the Five Books of Moses (Genesis,
Exodus, Leviticus, Numbers, Deuteronomy) or all together, "the
Pentateuch"). The other medium was oral formulation and oral
transmission. For long centuries, through prophets and sages, that
oral Torah was passed on until it was finally written down in

documents produced by sages, called rabbis, in the first six centuries of the common era.

The fundamental story of the oral Torah is represented in the following passage of Mishnah-tractate Avot, The Founders, which lists the chain of tradition from Sinai through to some of the principal authorities of the Mishnah of ca. 200 CE.

1:1A. Moses received Torah at Sinai and handed it on to Joshua, Joshua to elders, and elders to prophets.

B. And prophets handed it on to the men of the great assembly.

C. They said three things: (1) "Be prudent in judgment. (2) Raise up many disciples. (3) Make a fence for the Torah."

1:2A. Simeon the Righteous was one of the last survivors of the great assembly.

B. He would say: 'On three things does the world stand: (1) "On the Torah, (2) and on the Temple service, (3) and on deeds of loving kindness."

1:3A. Antigonos of Sokho received [the Torah] from Simeon the Righteous.

B. He would say, (1) "Do not be like servants who serve the master on condition of receiving a reward, (2) but [be] like servants who serve the master not on condition of receiving a reward. (3) And let the fear of Heaven be upon you."

1:4A. Yosé b. Yoezer of Seredah and Yosé b. Yohanan of Jerusalem received [it] from them.

B. Yosé b. Yoezer says, (1) "Let your house be a gathering place for sages. (2) And wallow in the dust of their feet. (3) And drink in their words with gusto."

1.5A. Yosé b. Yohanan of Jerusalem says, (1) "Let your house be wide open. (2) And seat the poor at your table, (3) And don't talk too much with women."

1:6A. Joshua B. Perahiah and Nittai the Arbelite received [it] from them.

B. Joshua b. Perahiah says, "Set up a master for yourself. (2) And get yourself a fellow disciple. (3) And give everybody the benefit of the doubt."

1:7A. Nittai the Arbelite says, (1) "Keep away from a bad neighbor. (2) And don't get involved with a wicked man. (3) And don't give up hope of retribution."

1:8A. Judah b. Tabbai and Simeon b. Shatah received [it] from them.

B. Judah b. Tabbai says, (1) "Don't make yourself like one of those who make advocacy before judges [while you yourself are judging a case]. (2) And when the litigants stand before you, regard them as guilty. (3) And when they leave you, regard them as acquitted, (when they have accepted your judgment)."

1:9A. Simeon b. Shatah says, (1) "Examine the witnesses with great care. (2) And watch what you say, (3) lest they learn from what you say how to lie."

1:10A. Shemaiah and Abtalion received [it] from them.

B. Shemaiah says, "(1) Love work. (2) Hate authority. (3) Don't get friendly with the government."

1:11A. Abtalion says, (1) "Sages, watch what you say, lest you become liable to the punishment of exile, and go into exile to a place of bad water, and disciples who follow you drink [bad water] and die, and the name of heaven be thereby profaned."

1:12A. Hillel and Shammai received [it] from them.

B. Hillel says, (1) "Be disciples of Aaron, loving peace and pursuing peace, loving people and drawing them near to the Torah."

1:13A. He would say [in Aramaic], (1) "A name made great is a name destroyed. (2) And one who does not add subtracts. (3) And who does not learn is liable to death. (4) And the one who uses the crown passes away."

1:14A. He would say, (1) "If I am not for myself, who is for me? (2) And when I am for myself, what am I? (3) And if not now, when?"

1:15A. Shammai says, (1) "Make your learning of Torah a fixed obligation. (2) Say little and do much. (3) Greet everybody cheerfully."

1:16 1A. Rabban Gamaliel says, (1) "Set up a master for yourself. (2) Avoid doubt. (3) Don't tithe by too much guesswork."

1:17 11A. Simeon his son says, "All my life I grew up among the sages, and I found nothing better for a person [the body] than silence. And not the learning is the main thing but the doing. And whoever talks too much causes sin."

1:18A. Rabban Simeon b. Gamaliel says, "On three things does the world stand: on justice, on truth, and on peace,"

B. "as it is said, Execute the judgment of truth and peace in your gates (Zech 8:16)."

Mishnah-Tractate Abot 1:1–18

There are two important aspects of this writing. First, the chain of authorities extends from Moses to sages of the first century CE who appear often in the pages of the Mishnah. So there is a clear claim that the Mishnah, and other writings in which these sages and their disciples appear, forms part of the Torah received by Moses at Sinai. Second, equally important, what these authorities say is not a reprise of Scripture but fresh material. While verses of the written Torah occur, they are cited as part of an independent writing, on which this writing calls for authority. This means that there is part of the Torah of Sinai that is not contained in Scripture, but that correlates with Scripture. Then how do we today have access, within the myth of this Judaism of the dual Torah, to the oral part of the Torah? According to the Judaism of the dual Torah, the oral Torah came to full expression and was written down in the writings of the sages of the Land of Israel ("the Holy Land," "Palestine") and of Babylonia between the first and the seventh centuries.

How do we know that this Judaism is different from all others? We know because of the doctrine of the other orally formulated and orally transmitted Torah, the memorized Torah. A brief survey of the principal documents of this Judaism suffices; later on we shall see how Torah figures in the more important of them.

The first document of this oral Torah was the Mishnah, a philosophical law code closed at about the year 200 CE. Further writings that fall into the classification of oral Torah include the Tosefta, a collection of supplements to the Mishnah's laws; the Talmud of the Land of Israel, a commentary to the Mishnah accomplished in the Land of Israel about 400 CE; and the Talmud of Babylonia, a second such commentary done in the Jewish communities of Babylonia about 600 CE. Over this same span of time, from ca. 200 through ca. 600, commentaries to the written Torah by the sages of the age – such as Sifra, Sifré to Numbers, Sifré to Deuteronomy, Genesis Rabbah, Leviticus Rabbah, and the like – were compiled. Called Midrash-compilations, these brought to bear upon the written Torah modes of thought and principles of the sages of the formative age. All of these documents, but especially the

Mishnah and its two great Talmuds containing the teachings of sages in late antiquity from the first through the sixth centuries of the Common Era, form that other oral Torah that, in accord with this Judaism, God revealed to Moses, called our rabbi ("Moshe rabbenu" in Hebrew), at Sinai. Now that we can define the Judaism whose story we follow in these pages, what can we say about its definition of the Torah? For there is more to "the Torah" than the books that encompass the written record of the originally oral Torah of Sinai – much more!

3

The Formation of the Written Torah:
Ezra and Pentateuchal Judaism

All Judaisms appeal to the same holy book, the Pentateuch or the Five Books of Moses. But, of course, each Judaism does what it will with the initial "Torah of Moses." For its part the Judaism of the dual Torah claims to derive from that same act of God's revelation that produced the written Torah. The reason the Pentateuch comes first in our consideration of the Torah of Judaism is not that it comes "in the beginning" and explains "where it all began." Simply, the Pentateuch forms one-half of the whole Torah of this Judaism. If, therefore, we wish to understand the initial character of the Judaism of the dual Torah, we do well to analyse the shape and structure that the written part of the Torah imparted to the whole of that Judaism.

Moreover, in all of the documents of the oral part of the Torah, the Pentateuch takes a primary position. It supplies texts to prove propositions, themes, and motifs to be worked out in terms of life later on, and it represents the court of appeal for disputes about what God requires.

Of course the Torah, as the Judaism of the dual Torah portrays God's revelation to Israel, does far more than merely paraphrase a given document. It is a religious system that comes to expression in the selection and representation of writings, but that is complete and wholly prior to and independent of any of these writings. What we learn from the Pentateuch concerns not its contribution to the Torah but how it attests, even in its initial form and condition, to a religious system that has selected it and focused upon it. That is a quite different question, one not of origins and beginnings but of shape and structure. It also is not a familiar question to people who are used to hearing opinion on whether or not something really happened or someone really lived. Our interest is not in one-time events of a remote past, but in how a religious system has framed its world-view and accounted for its way of life: the Pentateuch as a component of the Torah.

A reprise on the principal narrative motif of the Pentateuch is required, since the Pentateuch was read not only as a treasure of prooftexts but also as a sustained account of the life of Israel, the holy people, from beginning to happy ending in the land. To understand what follows, we must know that the Five Books of Moses (Genesis, Exodus, Leviticus, Numbers and Deuteronomy) speak of the creation of the world and God's identification of the children of Abraham, Isaac, and Jacob (who also was called "Israel") as God's people. Here we find two of the three principal parts of any Judaism: God and Israel. In that structure, Torah occupies the center: the people was born of the patriarchs and matriarchs but called to life at Sinai through the giving of the Torah. The story reaches its conclusion at the boundaries of the promised land, promised on the condition that the people, Israel, remain obedient to God by observing the requirements of the Torah. The land is what holds the whole together: possession of the land signifies obedience to the covenant through the Torah with God; loss of the land signifies disobedience to the covenant of the Torah and betrayal of God. That, then, is Pentateuchal Judaism portrayed in the simplest terms of its narrative.

One further element needs to be noted, that is, the stress Pentateuchal Judaism places upon the Temple, its offerings, its priests, and the relationship of Israel to God through the Temple. In the Pentateuchal narrative the Temple is represented by the tabernacle; a third of Exodus, all of Leviticus, a fourth of Numbers, and a large part of Deuteronomy center upon the Temple, the conditions of its cult, and the stipulations concerning possession of the Temple. So land and Temple go together: lose the one, lose the other.

The people are portrayed as taking shape in the land of Canaan, which was promised to Abraham and his seed and would be called the land of Israel; then going down to Egypt; then being freed of the bondage of Egypt by Moses, who led the people to Sinai; there receiving the Torah, consisting of the rules that were to govern the holy community and its service to God in the cult and Temple that would be built in time to come; and finally, encompassing the message that when Israel kept the contract or covenant made with God by the patriarchs and given substance at Sinai, God would favor Israel; when Israel did not keep the contract, God would punish Israel. This thumbnail sketch of the Torah suggests that the narrative is uniform and comes from the time of the events themselves.[1]

Where and when was the whole put together as we now have it? The answer to that question is important because when we read the Torah as a sustained narrative, from beginning to end (as we read it in the Judaism of the dual Torah), we are following the message of the whole in the composition, proportion, order, and sense that that final group of authors, editors, and compilers imparted. Then the message of the Pentateuch, encompassing diverse prior viewpoints and messages, is one that addresses the social world of the ultimate authorship, which has put everything together to say that one thing. The Pentateuch, as we now have it, is the work of an authorship of a particular period. To understand Pentateuchal Judaism and its contribution to the dual Torah, therefore, we require a further set of facts: what had happened before the age of formation and conclusion of the Torah, and what problems pressed upon the authorship of the Torah.

The facts are simple. The ancient Israelites settled the land before 1000 BCE and lived there for five centuries. The details of their history, culture, and religion need not detain us, because they do not define the history of Judaism. Only as these details were reshaped after a world-shaking event and formed into the Torah (and certain other writings) does the life of Israel from the conquest of the land to that

---

[1] The components of the Pentateuch play no role in our inquiry, nor are we interested in the history, before the final compilation of the Pentateuch as we know it, of those components. As a matter of fact, however, the Pentateuch consists of a variety of discrete writings, each marked by its own style and viewpoint. The writings that speak of the caste system – priests, Levites, Israelites – and of the Temple cult, the special tasks and duties and rights of the priests, for instance, are ascribed to a priestly authorship; these writers produced the Book of Leviticus and most of the Book of Numbers, as well as passages in the Book of Exodus that deal with the tabernacle. The entire Book of Deuteronomy, attributed to Moses as he looked back and narrated the story of the formation of Israel, represents an altogether different authorship with its own points of interest. One difference, for instance, is that the priestly writers in Leviticus take for granted that sacrifice to the Lord may take place in any appropriate holy place, while the authorship of the Book of Deuteronomy insists that sacrifice may take place only in the place that God will designate, by which Jerusalem's Temple is meant.

utter break – a caesura in time – matter to Judaism. What formed
Judaism was a sequence of two happenings which together form a
single event.

In 586 BCE the Temple of Jerusalem was destroyed by the expanding Babylonian Empire which had formed in the confluence of the
Tigris-Euphrates river, in the area of present-day Iraq near Baghdad.
The political classes of the Jewish state, the persons of economic
worth such as craftsmen, artisans, and others who counted, were
taken away to the homeland of the conquering empire. There they
were given land, and there they settled. To keep the populations of
the polyglot empire mixed, the Babylonians resettled other peoples
in the land of Israel, and these mixed with the Israelites who had not
been taken into exile. It was simply good public policy to form
heterogeneous populations in the theory of divide and conquer, and
that is what the Babylonians did.

Around three generations later, toward the end of the sixth century
BCE, the Babylonian Empire fell to the Persians, an Iranian people
whom we have already met briefly. As a matter of public policy their
emperor, Cyrus, sought to win the loyalty of his diverse empire
by returning populations, which had been removed from their
homelands by the Babylonians, to their points of origin. The Jews of
Babylonia were among those given the right to return to their
homeland. Very few of them did so. Those who returned made a
start at rebuilding the Temple. Some time later, in the middle of the
fifth century (450 BC), a successor to Cyrus allowed Nehemiah, a
high court official who was Jewish and a top bureaucrat and civil
servant, Ezra, to return to Jerusalem and, with the support of the
state, to rebuild the Temple and establish a Jewish government in
the province.

The two events – destruction and restoration – by themselves did
not produce a Judaic system known to us. But extensive writings –
for example, the later passages of Isaiah, Ezekiel, Jeremiah; the
formation of Joshua, Judges, Samuel, and Kings in their penultimate
form – all were composed in light of the destruction and, in the case
of Isaiah 40–60ff., the restoration. A reconsideration of the whole of
Israel's history in relationship to the land, however, such as forms
the centerpiece of the Pentateuchal narrative read from beginning
to end as a linear account, awaited the restoration. Then exile and
return formed a whole, and the message of the parts was reshaped

as they formed a whole not only greater than but different from the sum of the parts.

In the Pentateuchal revision, these two events – destruction and restoration – come together as "exile and return" and are framed in terms as mythic and transcendent in their context and as rich and intense in their human messages as "the Holocaust and Redemption" of contemporary Judaism. In making such a comparison, however, we turn matters on their head. For, as we shall now see, the historical events of 586 and 450 are transformed in the Pentateuch's picture of the history and destiny of Israel into that generative myth of exile and return that imparted to the Judaism of the dual Torah its critical tension. The "if . . . then" that explains the real world of actualities and events finds its dynamic in the Pentateuchal message: loss of the land follows from violation of the Torah; possession of the land depends upon keeping the Torah; and the land is not a given but a gift, one that can be taken away. All of this came to definitive expression in the matter of possession or loss of the Temple.

With the destruction of the Temple in 586 followed by the return to Zion in the beginning of the fifth century, the human situation and the political actualities of Israel came to concrete expression: death and renewal addressed the everyday life of ordinary folk as much as exile and return spoke to the nation in its land. What are the rules that define the conditions of life of the Israelite and the rules governing the fortunes of Israel as a social, political entity? The story of the beginnings, which the Pentateuch tells, emphasizes two points:

1. The formation of Israel and its covenant with God, time and again insisting on the holiness of Israel and its separateness from the other peoples;

2. The conditional possession of the land as the mark of the covenant.

The people had the land not as a given but as a gift. As long as they kept the covenant, the land would be theirs and they would prosper in it. If the people violated the Torah or the conditions of the covenant, they would lose the land. The relevant texts are Leviticus 26 and Deuteronomy 32. However, if you review the narrative of Genesis and its account of how the people took shape and got the land, you will see that the relationship of Israel to the land is the leitmotif throughout. Everything else depends upon it. When you get to the land you build the Temple. When you get to the land you obey these laws. When you get to the land you form a godly society and carry out the Torah. So the condition of the people dictates their right to the land, and in losing the land, the people is warned to keep the Torah and the conditions that it sets forth. Therefore, in recovering the land, the people enjoy a redemption that is conditional: not a given but a gift.

Read by itself, the Pentateuch proves particularly pertinent to an Israel in possession of the land and in control of the Temple. Appeals, then, to obedience to the Torah invoke the evidences of divine grace near at hand. While the symbol of the Torah in that context is required, it is not sufficient for Pentateuchal Judaism to accomplish its goals. If I had to choose a symbol critical to Pentateuchal Judaism among the three available to all Judaisms– God, Torah, Israel – I should choose the symbol of Israel. The critical issue of the Pentateuchal system is the condition that governs Israel's life on the land – that above all. In position and proportion, the symbol of the Torah is subordinated to the symbol of the holy people, which is principal actor in the drama formed of the tension between God's will and Israel's will, a drama acted out upon the stage of the land.

How does Israel take center stage? Throughout the Torah's narrative – in Genesis, where the patriarchs go "home" to Babylonia for their women; in Leviticus, with its exclusion of the Canaanites whom "the land vomited out" because of their wickedness; in Deuteronomy, with its command to wipe out some groups and to proscribe marriage with others – the stress is the same: form high walls between Israel and its nearest neighbors. The stress on exclusion of the neighbors from the group and of the group from the neighbors in fact runs contrary to the situation of ancient Israel. For unmarked frontiers of culture and the constant giving and receiving among diverse groups generally characterize the situation of ancient times.

Engagement with the definition of Israel and the protection of Israel's integrity persisted. The reason is that the stress on differentiation, yielding a preoccupation with self-definition, contradicted the social facts that defined the political circumstances of the nation. In the time when the Pentateuch was being formed, Israel was deeply affected by the shifts and changes in social, cultural, and political life and institutions. A century and a half after the formation of the Pentateuch under Ezra and Nehemiah, when the Greeks under

Alexander the Great conquered the entire Middle East (ca. 320 BCE) and incorporated the land of Israel into the international Hellenistic culture, the problem of self-definition came to renewed expression. When the war of independence fought by the Jews under the leadership of the Maccabees (ca. 160 BCE) produced an independent state for a brief period, that state found itself under the government of a court that accommodated itself to the international style of politics and culture. So what was different? What made Israel separate and secure on its land and in its national identity?

In that protracted moment of confusion and change the heritage of the Five Books of Moses came to closure. Moreover, the same situation persisted that had marked the age in which the Pentateuch had delivered its message, answering with self-evidently valid responses the urgent question of the nation's existence. So we understand the persistence of the Pentateuchal system for a long time – for as long as possession of the land defined the existential facts of Israel's life, and as long as the faithful service of God by the priests in the Temple of Jerusalem marked the presence and promise of God's grace for Israel, the people, in the land of Israel. It is when the facts of life shifted that the Pentateuchal component of the one whole Torah of Moses was joined with the oral component of that same Torah. I am referring to the time of the destruction of the Temple of Jerusalem in 70 and the caesura marked by the defeat of the Jews in the war "three generations later," in 132–135, to regain the Temple. Then but only then compelling issues arose that lay beyond the mythic structure of the received Pentateuchal system. Israel *not* in possession of both the land and the Temple, the land held by both Israel and outsiders – that situation, which persisted from 70 to 1948, redefined the social realities in so ambiguous a way that a new medium of classification was required. And the Torah would and did expand to accord with the social world at hand. The Judaism of the dual Torah, then, over the next half-millennium, gained the other, the oral Torah.

As we reach the end of the period in which the written part of the Torah had served pretty much on its own, we ask: Can we identify the fundamental contribution to the Torah made by the compilers of the Pentateuch? Among the three principal symbols of any Judaism, we found that the Pentateuch focuses upon Israel or the social component. How was that opaque symbol shaped and formed to receive and refract the light of the common life? The principal givens of the Pentateuchal Torah's paradigm take shape around Israel's heightened sense of its own social reality, its status as an elected people standing in a contractual or covenantal relationship with God, and the whole worked out through the relationship of Israel to the land of Israel, propositions of both the Torah and the historical and prophetic writings of the century beyond 586.

These data refer to facts, to be sure, but they derive not from the data of Israel's common life in Babylonia or in the land of Israel but from the choices of the system-builders themselves. For the framers of the system selected the events they would deem consequential. They did not simply narrate things that had happened to pretty much everyone. That act of selection forms a decision dictated by a prior religious system, a Judaism in being, among the available choices supplied by prior experience and the writing down of that experience. Why do I insist on the proposition that the Pentateuch, to begin with, formed a construct and expressed the choices of its framers rather than presenting an account of things that had happened in the time of its compilation? The reason is simple. From the perspective of a vast population of Israel, Jews who remained in the land and Jews who never left Babylonia, the system spoke of events that had simply never happened.

Consider the Jews who remained in the land after 586 or those who remained in Babylonia after Cyrus's decree permitted the return to Zion. For both groups, for different reasons, there was no alienation and, consequently, no reconciliation. The normative corresponded to the merely normal: life like any other nation wherever it happened to locate itself. True, treating exile and return as normative imparted to the exile the critical and definitive position. It marked Israel as special, elect, subject to the rules of the covenant and its stipulations. But for much of Israel, some system other than the system of the normative alienation constructed by the Judaism of the Torah would have to have enjoyed the self-evidence that, for exiles who returned, the system of the Torah possessed. For those who did not return to Zion, the urgent question of exile and return, the self-evidently valid response of election and covenant, bore slight relevance, asked no questions worth asking, and provided no answers worth believing.

When we want an example of a religious system creating a society, we can find few better instances than the power of the conception of

Israel expressed in the Pentateuch and associated writings. The heightened reality and the intense focus on the identification of the nation as extraordinary, as expressed in these writings, represents only one possible picture of the meaning of events from 586 onward. We do not have access, it seems, except to the system of the Torah and the prophetic and historical writings that were framed by the priests and given definitive statement under the auspices of the Iranian's Jewish viceroy in Jerusalem, Nehemiah, with Ezra as counselor.

What happened in 586 and after, and what the paradigm fabricated out of what happened, do not correspond. Scripture said, in both the Torah and the prophetic-historical books, that Israel suffered through exile, atoned, attained reconciliation, and renewed the covenant with God as signified by the return to Zion and the rebuilding of the Temple. Although only a minority of "Israel" had, in fact, undergone these experiences, the Judaic system of the Torah nevertheless made the experience of alienation and reconciliation normative. Religion (the particular Judaism at hand) therefore did more than merely recapitulate resentment; it precipitated it by selecting as events only a narrow sample of what had happened and by imparting to that selection of events meanings pertinent to only a few.

In its original statement, the system of the Torah after 586 did not merely describe things that had actually happened, normal events so to speak, but rendered them normative and mythic, turning an experience into a paradigm of experience. Let me state the important point in a simple way:

1. The paradigm began as a paradigm, not as a set of actual events transformed into a normative pattern;

2. The conclusions generated by the paradigm derived not from reflection on things that happened but from the logic of the paradigm;

3. That same paradigm created expectations that could not be met and consequently renewed the resentment captured by the myth of exile; at the same time it set the conditions for remission of resentment, thus resolving the crisis of exile with the promise of return;

4. This self-generating, self-renewing paradigm formed the self-fulfilling prophecy that all Judaisms have offered as the generative tension and critical symbolic structure of their systems.

The paradigm that imparted its imprint on the history of the day did not emerge from and was not generated by the events of the age. First came the system, its world-view, and its way of life, formed whole we know not where or by whom. Then came the selection by the system of consequential events and their patterning into systemic propositions. Finally, at a third stage of indeterminate length, came the formation and composition of the canon that would express the logic of the system and state those "events" that the system would select or invent for its own expression. Since chief among the propositions of the system is the notion of the election of Israel effected in the covenant, we may say that, systemically speaking, Israel – the Israel of the Torah and historical-prophetic books of the sixth and fifth centuries – selected itself. The system created the paradigm of the society that had gone into exile and come back home. Moreover, the system also cut its own orders, the contract or covenant that certified not election but self-selection.

At the foundation of the original and generative Judaic paradigm, that is, the account of the sequence of events from 586 when the Israelites were exiled to Babylonia to 450 when they had returned to Zion and rebuilt the Temple, we find history systemically selected, therefore invented, but not described. This would really not matter – for everyone understands the mythopoeic (myth-creating) power of belief – except for one thing. I maintain that a particular experience, transformed by a religious system into a paradigm of the life of the social group, became normative and therefore generative. That particular experience *itself* happened in the minds and imaginations of the authorships of Scripture, not in the concrete life or in the politics and society of Israel in its land and in exile.

No one, of course, imagined that the Temple lay in ruins. But as to its restoration and reconstruction, people clearly differed, as the incessant complaints of the post-exilic prophets about the neglected condition of the altar attest. No one denied that some of Israel had stayed at home and that some had gone into exile. But as to the exclusion of those who had stayed at home and not undergone the normative experience of alienation and return, opinion surely differed, since it was only by force that the dissolution of families was effected. The same applies to a long list of systemic givens, none of them matters of self-evidence except to those to whom they were self-evident. Thus it is Scripture – and Scripture alone – that says that

Israel died and was reborn, was punished through exile and then forgiven, and therefore to be *Israel* is, in a genealogical sense, to have gone into exile and returned to Zion.

The contribution of the Pentateuch to the Judaism of the dual Torah is therefore not only the reworking of the symbols of God and Israel upon the ground of the holy land. It is the much more profound, definitive reality of the power of Scripture – the Torah – to convey and also to create the very structure and system within which the other formative symbols, God and Israel, would find their place. The fact that the compilers of the Pentateuch were also the ones who chose, selected, and arranged facts to convey the story of God's and Israel's engagement within the land and Temple provides the key to all that would happen to the Torah. Those who would in time inherit and hand on the Torah (no longer the Pentateuch as Ezra compiled it) would be the ones to shape and rework the Torah. It would be the symbol of the Torah that would occupy the center of the drama and dynamic of Judaic systems, whether on stage or in the wings.

Briefly, what happened to people does not correspond to what people were told had happened. Most people stayed in Babylonia after 586, but called it exile. A few migrated to Jerusalem, where they found themselves a tiny minority among a larger group of Israelites whose ways they found improper; but they told themselves they had come "home," that they had "returned to Zion." Still, by their own word they did not find much familiar about this "home" of theirs, since most of the people who lived there followed rules the returnees declared alien. On both sides, the "exiles" and those who had come "home," the systemic paradigm transformed what was happening into something else.

Not only the Judaism of the dual Torah, but all other Judaic systems later on would rehearse in one way or another this Pentateuchal Judaism. We must therefore ask ourselves why the paradigm persisted long after the political facts had shifted dramatically, indeed, had ceased to pertain at all. The answer to that question will also tell us why, in the Judaism of the dual Torah, the received paradigm would govern, even while given other points of emphasis and interest altogether.

The answer is in two parts. First, all Judaisms would accord pride of place to the Pentateuch, saying through it whatever they wished to say. Second, the Pentateuch, however twisted and turned, still set forth a single, profound paradigm of human experience. That explains how and why the experience to which it originally constituted a profound and systematic response was recapitulated, age after age, through the reading and authoritative exegesis of the original Scripture that preserved and portrayed it: "Your descendants will be aliens living in a land that is not theirs . . . but I will punish that nation whose slaves they are, and after that they shall come out with great possessions" (Gen. 15:13–14).

The persistence of the priests' Judaism as the self-evidently valid explanation of Israel's life derives from two facts. The Judaic system, devised in the Pentateuch by the priests, retained its power of self-evidence in that that system, in its basic structure, addressed *and created* a continuing and chronic social fact of Israel's life. When the world imposed upon Jewry questions of a different order, Jews would go in search of more answers – an additional Torah (hence the formation of the Judaism of the dual Torah) – and even different answers. Still, the world was constructed in peoples' vision through that original perspective created in the aftermath of destruction and restoration, that is, seeing the world as a gift instead of a given, themselves as chosen for a life of special suffering but also special reward. The generative tension, precipitated by the interpretation of the Jews' life as exile and return (the critical center of the Torah of Moses), persisted. Therefore the urgent question answered by the Torah retained its original character and definition, and the self-evidently valid answer, read in the synagogue every Sabbath morning as well as on Monday and on Thursday, retained its relevance. The notion of loss and restoration joined to the recognition in the here and now of the danger of a further loss also confirmed that the priests' authoritative answer would not lose its power to endure and to persuade. People were thus able to see what was not always there because, through the Torah of Moses, they were taught to.

The question of the human condition phrased in terms of exile and return persisted because Scripture kept reminding people to ask that question. For a small, uncertain people, captured by a vision of distant horizons, a mere speck on the crowded plain of humanity, such a message was powerful and immediate as a map of meaning. The Pentateuch encapsulated as normative and recurrent the experience of the loss and recovery of the land and of political sovereignty. Because of its (in its mind) amazing experience, Israel had attained a self-conscious continuous existence in a single place under a long-term government that was denied to others (and had been denied Israel before 586). There was nothing to be celebrated or at least taken for granted in the life of a nation that had ceased to be a nation on its own land, and then once more had regained that once-normal (now abnormal) condition. The Torah, as set forth in the stage marked by the Pentateuch, presented the system that accounted for the death and resurrection of Israel, the Jewish people. In time to come that written Torah would be joined by the oral Torah, which reshaped matters into an account of renewal in the aftermath of the destruction through sanctification now, and salvation at the end of time. The first stage in the formation of the dual Torah attended to sanctification, the second to salvation.

4

The Initial System of the Dual Torah:
The Mishnah and Israel's Sanctification

The Mishnah shows us the next stage in the development of the dual Torah. Its origins belong to the aftermath of defeat in the First War against Rome, in 70 CE, which produced the destruction of the Temple and the loss of Jerusalem; similarly also in the Second War against Rome, 132 to 135, which sealed the fate of the Temple and Jerusalem for years to come. Later on the Mishnah was accorded status as a principal part of the oral tradition that formed half of the one whole Torah received by Moses at Sinai; it responded to issues of the destruction of the Temple and subsequent defeat in the failed war for restoration. After the destruction in 70 CE and the still more disheartening defeat of 135, the Mishnah's sages worked out a Judaism without a Temple and a cult, producing a system of sanctification focused on the holiness of the priesthood, the cultic festivals, the Temple and its sacrifices, and on the rules for protecting that holiness from levitical uncleanness – four of the six divisions of the Mishnah on a single theme.

Why is the Mishnah important in the Torah? Because the Judaism of the dual Torah identifies the Mishnah as its initial writing, a philosophical law code brought to closure about 200 CE. All writings between the written Torah (its beginnings were assigned to Sinai about 1200 BCE, followed by the prophetic books and hagiographa, concluding with Haggai, Malachi, and Zechariah) and the advent of the Mishnah centuries later, were ignored. In this account of the history of the Judaism of the dual Torah, based on the story of Torah through the ages, we follow the above chronological scheme. We therefore leap from the completion of the written Torah in about 450

BCE by Ezra directly to the framing of the first writing identified as part of the oral Torah.

If the time gap seems formidable (nearly seven hundred years) the linear historical continuity in intellectual terms proves still more compelling. For the Mishnah addressed the condition of Israel in relationship to God and to the land in the aftermath of the radical change effected by the Temple's destruction and the loss of Jerusalem. From the time of Ezra and the building of the Second Temple down to the destruction of the same Temple, in the view of the Judaism of the dual Torah, nothing happened drastically to change the givens of Israel's condition on earth, and therefore also in heaven.

The Temple in Jerusalem, where sacrifices were offered to God, formed the focus of Pentateuchal Judaism. The lives of the patriarchs repeatedly drew them into relationship with the sacrificial cult in various holy places, but especially in Jerusalem. The laws of the Torah dealt in detail with the sacrifices, priests, maintenance of the priestly caste, and other cultic matters. The cycle of holy time was marked by sacrifice. So the power of the Torah, composed in this time, was in its control of the Temple. The Temple cult, with its total exclusion of non-Israelites from participation and cultic commensality, raised high the walls of separation and underlined such distinctiveness as already existed. The life of Israel flowed from the altar; what made Israel Israel was the center, the altar. And in 70 CE, in the course of a war fought by Jews against Roman rule in the land of Israel, Jerusalem fell and the Temple, except for its western wall, was destroyed. How were the faithful to deal with the issues of Israel's life in the land now that conditions had so radically changed?

The question would be formulated in terms of sanctification. Israel as social entity was designated as different, separate, and holy, and the sanctification of holy Israel was commemorated and enacted in the Temple. The offerings lost, the priesthood or the holy caste within Israel bereft of its sacred labors, the building in ruins, the holy city no longer accessible – what was now the locus of sanctification? The authorship of the Mishnah, between 70 and 200, worked out the self-evidently valid answer to the compelling question raised by the events of 70 and 132 to 135. The answer was that Israel in the land remained in a holy place and, more important, Israel itself, the holy people, endured as holy. But how could that sanctification be expressed and brought to full realization? If it could not be expressed in the Temple and its sacrifices, it must be realized in the everyday life of Israel in the holy land itself.

The second phase in the formation of the Judaism of the dual Torah thus took the received issue of sanctification as the center of its interest and worked out a compelling and acutely relevant response to the crisis of the day. The next phase in the unfolding of this same history would address an urgent crisis and respond by reshaping the received Torah, a continuous and linear history.

What should be sanctified now, as the Temple had been through its cult? It would have to be the one locus of sanctification that endured beyond 70, which was the holy people itself. That people's life, on the holy land at the start but later everywhere the people lived, would be made holy. Holy meant separate and distinct from the ordinary. Consequently the chronic question of who is a Jew and what is Israel would find its self-evidently valid response in the same categories as the Pentateuchal system had defined for itself. The stress of the Judaism of the dual Torah (framed by sages and hence called "rabbinic Judaism") on the sanctification of the home and the paradigmatic power of the Temple for the home, points to a more extreme position within the priestly paradigm than that of the priests who wrote parts of Exodus, Leviticus, and Numbers. What the priests wanted for the Temple, the dual Torah wanted for the community Israel at large. The premise of the written Torah, we recall, rested on a simple allegation: if Israel observed the terms of the covenant of a sanctified life, it would enjoy prosperity in a serene land and a national life outside of history.

The traumatic event of annihilation and rebirth portrayed by the reworking of the ancient Israelite writings into the Pentateuch, and the death and resurrection of the nation, brought about yearning for one thing above all else: no more, or never again. The picture of what had happened presented solace. That is why people wanted to accept the portrait of their world. The restoration gave Israel a second chance at life. But Israel could also rely on knowledge of the rules that governed its national life, those of the Torah and its repeated allegations of an agreement or covenant between Israel and God, to make certain there would be no more experiences of exile and alienation (whether or not followed by reconciliation and restoration). This same paradigm prevailed in the framing of the Judaism of the dual Torah. What shifted was the redefinition of salvation from the here and now to the end of time. That change, of course, was not only plausible; it was necessary in light of the catastrophe at hand.

The Mishnah is a six-part code of descriptive rules. The six divisions are: 1. agricultural rules; 2. laws governing appointed times or seasons, for example, Sabbaths and festivals; 3. laws on the transfer of women and property along with the deeding of women from one man (father) to another (husband); 4. the system of civil and criminal law, corresponding to what we today regard as the "legal system;" 5. laws for the conduct of the cult and the Temple; and 6. laws on the preservation of cultic purity both in the Temple and under certain domestic circumstances, with special reference to the table and bed. To see what the Mishnah's framers contributed to the Torah, we must first describe and briefly interpret the six components of the Mishnah's system. A central concern in most of the document concerns sanctification of the everyday in relationship to the Temple and its cult.

The critical issue in economic life, which really means farming, is dealt with in the first division in two parts. First, Israel as tenant on God's holy land maintains the property in the ways God requires, keeping the rules which mark the land and its crops as holy. Next, the hour at which the sanctification of the land comes to form a critical mass, namely, when the crops ripen, is a moment filled with danger and heightened holiness. Israel's will affects the crops, marking a part of them holy and the rest of them available for common use. The human will is determinative in the process of sanctification.

According to the Mishnah's second division, at certain appointed times spaces of the land are set apart as holy in yet another way. The center of the land and the focus of its sanctification is the Temple. There the produce of the land is received and given back to God, the one who created and sanctified the land. At these unusual moments of sanctification, the inhabitants of the land in their respective villages enter a state of spatial sanctification. That is to say, the village boundaries mark off holy space, within which one must remain during the holy time. This is expressed in two ways. First, the Temple itself observes and expresses the special, recurring holy time. Second, the villages of the land are brought into alignment with the Temple, forming a complement and completion to the

Temple's sacred being. The advent of the appointed times precipitates a spatial reordering of the land so that the boundaries of the
sacred are matched and mirrored in village and in Temple. At the
heightened holiness marked by these moments of appointed times,
therefore, the occasion for an affective sanctification is worked out.
Like the harvest, the advent of an appointed time or a pilgrim festival
or a sacred season, is made to express that regular, orderly, and
predictable sort of sanctification for Israel which the system as a
whole seeks.

The counterpart of the divisions of agriculture and appointed
times, which concern the farm and the village, are the fifth and sixth
divisions, namely, holy things and purities. These deal with the
Temple and the cult. So we contrast the everyday and the ordinary
of the first two divisions with opposites, the extraordinary and the
holy. The two of course match as complementary opposites.

The fifth division is about the Temple on ordinary days. As the
locus of sanctification, it functions in an entirely routine, trustworthy,
and punctilious manner. The one element which may unsettle
matters is the intention and will of the human actor, but these are
subjected to carefully prescribed limitations and remedies.

The division of holy things generates its companion, the sixth
division, regarding cultic cleanness or purities. The relationship
between the two resembles that between agriculture and appointed
times. The former is locative, the latter utopian; the former deals
with the fields, the latter with the interplay between fields and altar.

The sixth division also, after speaking of the one place of the
Temple, addresses the cleanness which pertains to every place. A
system of cleanness – one that takes into account what imparts
uncleanness and how, together with what is subject to uncleanness
and how it is overcome – is again fully expressed in response to the
participation of the human will. Without the wish and act of a human
being, the system does not function; it is inert. Sources of uncleanness,
which come naturally and not by volition, and modes of purification,
which work naturally and not by human intervention, remain inert
until human will has imparted susceptibility to uncleanness, that is,
until it has introduced into the system that food and drink, bed, pot,
chair, and pan, which form the focus of the system. The movement
from sanctification to uncleanness takes place when human will and
work precipitate it.

The third and fourth divisions, on women and damages, take their place in the structure of the whole by showing the congruence, within the larger framework of regularity and order, of human concerns of family and farm, politics, and workaday transactions among ordinary people. Without attending to these matters, the Mishnah's system does not encompass what, at its foundations, it is meant to comprehend and order. What is at issue is fully cogent with the rest. In the case of women, the third division, attention focuses upon the point of disorder marked by the transfer of that disordering anomaly, woman, from the regular status provided by one man to the equally trustworthy status provided by another. That is the point at which the Mishnah's interests are aroused: once more, predictably, the moment of disorder. In the case of damages, the fourth division, there are two important concerns. First, there is the paramount interest in preventing, as far as possible, the disorderly rise of one person and fall of another, and in sustaining the status quo of the economy, house, and household of Israel (the holy society) in eternal stasis. Second, there is the necessary concomitant in the provision of a system of political institutions to carry out the laws which preserve the balance and steady state of persons.

Now we ask ourselves: Precisely what systemic message comes to expression in the medium of the language just described? The system of the Mishnah delivers the message that through order – through the reordering of Israelite life – Israel attains that sanctification that inheres in its very being. From our perspective upon the whole, let us turn to the details and survey the several parts of the system, the six divisions and their sixty-two tractates.[1] In this way we gain a precise picture of how the authorship of the Mishnah has addressed the question of sanctification in the absence of Temple, officiating priesthood, and cult.

The Division of Agriculture treats two topics: 1. the production of crops according to the scriptural rules on the subject, and 2. payment of the required offerings and tithes to the priests, Levites, and poor. The principal point of the division is that the land is holy because God has a claim both upon it and upon what it produces. God's claim must be honored by setting aside a portion of the produce for

---

[1] Excluding tractate Avot, The Fathers, which, while printed with the Mishnah, was composed a generation or two later.

those for whom God has designated it. God's ownership must be acknowledged by observing the rules God has laid down for use of the land. In sum, the division is divided along these lines: 1. rules for producing crops in a state of holiness – tractates *Kilayim, Shebiit, Orlah*; 2. rules for disposing of crops in accord with the rules of holiness – tractates *Peah, Demai, Terumot, Maaserot, Maaser Sheni, Hallah, Bikkurim, Berakhot*.

The Division of Appointed Times forms a system in which the advent of a holy day, like the Sabbath of creation, sanctifies the life of the Israelite village by imposing rules on the village that are modeled on those of the Temple. The purpose of the system is to bring into alignment the moment of sanctification of the village and the life of the home with the moment of sanctification of the Temple on those same occasions or appointed times. The underlying and generative theory of the system is that the village is a mirror image of the Temple. If things are done one way in the Temple, they will be done the opposite way in the village. Together the village and the Temple, on the occasion of the holy day, form a single continuum, a completed creation awaiting sanctification.

The division is made up of two quite distinct sets of materials. First, it addresses what one does in the sacred space of the Temple on the occasion of sacred time, as distinct from what one does in that same sacred space on ordinary, undifferentiated days (a subject which is worked out in Holy Things). Second, the division defines how, on the occasion of the holy day, one creates a corresponding space in one's own circumstance, and what one does within that space during sacred time. The issue of the Temple and cult on the special occasion of festivals is treated in tractates *Pesahim, Sheqalim, Yoma, Sukkah,* and *Hagigah*. Three further tractates, *Rosh Hashshanah, Taanit,* and *Megillah*, are necessary to complete the discussion. The matter of the rigid definition of the outlines in the village, of a sacred space, delineated by the limits within which one may move on the Sabbath and festival, and of the specification of those things which one may not do within that space in sacred time, is in *Shabbat, Erubin, Besah,* and *Moed Qatan*. While the twelve tractates of the division appear to fall into two distinct groups, joined merely by a common theme, they in fact relate through a shared, generative metaphor. That metaphor is the comparison of the spatial life of the Temple to the spatial life of the village, with activities and restrictions to be specified for each, upon the common occasion of the Sabbath or festival. The Mishnah's purpose is to correlate the sanctity of the Temple, as defined by the holy day, with the restrictions of space and of action which make the life of the village different and holy.

The Division of Women defines women in the social economy of Israel's supernatural and natural reality. Women acquire definition wholly in relationship to men, who impart form to the Israelite social economy. The status of women is effected through both supernatural and natural, this-worldly action. What man and woman do on earth provokes a response in heaven, and the correspondences are perfect. So women are defined and secured both in heaven and on earth, and that position is always and invariably relative to men. The principal interest for the Mishnah is the point at which a woman becomes, and ceases to be, holy to a particular man, that is, enters and leaves the marital union. These transfers of women are the dangerous and disorderly points in the relationship of woman to man, and therefore, the Mishnah states, to society as well.

Discussion of the formation of marriage is contained in *Qiddushin* and *Ketubot*, as well as in *Yebamot*. The rules for the duration of the marriage are scattered throughout, but derive especially from parts of *Ketubot, Nedarim,* and *Nazir*, on the one side, and the paramount unit of *Sotah*, on the other. Dissolution of marriage is dealt with in *Gittin*, as well as in *Yebamot*. We see clearly, therefore, that important overall are issues of the transfer of property, along with women, covered in *Ketubot* and to some measure in *Qiddushin*, and the proper documentation of the transfer of women and property, treated in *Ketubot* and *Gittin*. The critical issues turn upon legal documents, such as writs of divorce, and legal recognition of changes in the ownership of property – for example, through the collection of the settlement of a marriage contract by a widow, through the provision of a dowry, or through the disposition of the property of a woman during the period in which she is married. Within this orderly world of documentary and procedural concerns, a place is made for the disorderly conception of the marriage not formed by human volition but decreed in heaven, the levirate connection. *Yebamot* states that supernature sanctifies a woman to a man (under the conditions of the levirate connection). What it says by indirection is that man sanctifies too: man, like God, can sanctify that relationship between a man and a woman and can also effect the cessation of the sanctity of that same relationship. Five of the seven tractates of the Division of Women are devoted to the formation and dissolution of the marital bond. Of them, three treat what is done by man here on earth, that is, formation of a marital bond through betrothal and marriage contract and dissolution through divorce and its consequences: *Qiddushin*, *Ketubot*, and *Gittin*. One of them is devoted to what is done by woman here on earth: *Sotah*. And *Yebamot*, greatest of the seven in size and in formal and substantive brilliance, deals with the corresponding heavenly intervention into the formation and end of a marriage: the effect of death upon both forming the marital bond and dissolving it. The other two tractates, *Nedarim* and *Nazir*, draw into one the two realms of reality, heaven and earth, as they work out the effects of vows – perhaps because vows taken by women and subject to the confirmation or abrogation of the father or husband make a deep impact upon the marital life of the woman who has taken them.

The Division of Damages comprises two subsystems, which fit together in a logical way. One presents rules for the normal conduct of civil society. These cover commerce, trade, real estate, and other matters of everyday intercourse, as well as mishaps, such as damages by chattels and persons, fraud, overcharge, interest, and the like, in that same context of everyday social life. The other describes the institutions governing the normal conduct of civil society, that is, courts of administration and the penalties at the disposal of the government for the enforcement of the law. The two form a single, tight, and systematic dissertation on the nature of Israelite society and its economic, social, and political relationships, as the Mishnah envisages them.

The main point of the first of the two parts of the division is expressed in the sustained unfolding of the three *Babas* (*Baba Qamma*, *Baba Mesia*, and *Baba Batra*), that is, that it is the task of society to maintain perfect stasis, to preserve the prevailing situation, and to secure the stability of all relationships. To this end, in the interchanges of buying and selling, giving and taking, borrowing and lending, it is important that there be an essential equality of interchange. No party in the end should have more than at the outset, and none should be the victim of a sizable shift in fortune and circumstance. All parties' rights to and in this stable and unchanging economy of society are to be preserved. When the condition of a person is violated, the law will secure the restoration of the antecedent status as far as possible.

An appropriate appendix to the *Babas* is *Abodah Zarah*, which deals with the orderly governance of transactions and relationships between Israelite society and the outside world, the realm of idolatry, and relationships which are subject to certain special considerations. Israelites were not to derive benefit (that is, through commercial transactions) from anything that had served in the worship of an idol. Consequently commercial transactions suffered limitations because of extrinsic considerations of cultic taboos. While these covered both special occasions (for example, fairs and festivals of idolatry) and general matters (what Israelites may buy and sell) the main practical illustrations of the principles of the matter pertain to wine. The Mishnah supposes that gentiles routinely make use, for a libation, of a drop of any sort of wine to which they have access. It therefore is taken for granted that wine over which gentiles have had control is forbidden for Israelite use, and also that such wine is prohibited for Israelites to buy and sell. This other matter – ordinary everyday relationships with the gentile world with special reference to trade and commerce – concludes what the Mishnah has to say about all those matters of civil and criminal law which together define everyday relationships within the Israelite nation, and between that nation and all others in the world among whom, in Palestine as abroad, they lived side by side.

The other part of the division describes the institutions of Israelite government and politics. First, it describes the institutions and their jurisdiction, with reference to courts, conceived as both judicial and administrative agencies; second, it provides an extensive discussion of criminal penalties. The penalties are three: death, banishment, and flogging. There are four ways by which a person convicted of a capital crime may be put to death. The Mishnah organizes a vast amount of information regarding which capital crimes are punishable by which of the four modes of execution. That information is alleged to derive from Scripture. But the facts are many, and the relevant verses few. What the Mishnah clearly contributes to this exercise is a first-rate piece of organization and elucidation of available facts. Where the facts come from we do not know. The Mishnah-tractate *Sanhedrin* further describes the way in which trials are conducted in both monetary and capital cases and pays attention to the possibilities of perjury. The matter of banishment brings the Mishnah to a rather routine restatement regarding flogging, and application of that mode of punishment concludes the discussion. Our selection from the Mishnah derives from Mishnah-tractate *Sanhedrin* because that is where the reward and punishment involved in eternal life, or life in the world to come, takes its place within the larger category of penalty for violating the law of the Torah.

The character and interests of the Division of Damages present probative evidence of the larger program of the philosophers of the Mishnah. Their intention is to create nothing less than a full-scale Israelite government, subject to the administration of sages. This government is fully supplied with a constitution and bylaws (*Sanhedrin, Makkot*). It makes provision for a court system and procedures (*Shebuot, Sanhedrin, Makkot*), as well as a full set of laws governing civil society (*Baba Qamma, Baba Mesia, Baba Batra*) and criminal justice (*Sanhedrin, Makkot*). This government, moreover, mediates between its own community and the outside ("pagan") world. Through its system of laws it expresses its judgment of the others and at the same time defines, protects, and defends its own society and social frontiers (*Abodah Zarah*). It even makes provision for procedures of remission to expiate its own errors (Horayot).

The Division of Holy Things presents a system of sacrifice and sanctuary, that is, matters concerning the praxis of the altar and maintenance of the sanctuary. The praxis of the altar involves sacrifice and things set aside for sacrifice, thus deemed consecrated. *Zebahim* and part of *Hullin, Menahot, Temurah, Keritot*, part of *Meilah, Tamid*, and *Qinnim* deal with these matters. The maintenance of the sanctuary (inclusive of the personnel) is dealt with in *Bekhorot, Arakhin*, part of *Meilah, Middot*, and part of *Hullin*. Viewed from a distance, therefore, the division's eleven tractates divide themselves up into the following groups (in parentheses are tractates containing relevant materials): 1. rules for the altar and the praxis of the cult – *Zebahim, Menahot, Hullin, Keritot, Tamid, Qinnim (Bekhorot, Meilah)*; 2. rules for the altar and the animals set aside for the cult – *Arakhin, Temurah, Meilah (Bekhorot)*; and 3. rules for the altar and support of the Temple staff and buildings – *Bekhorot, Middot (Hullin, Arakhin, Meilah, Tamid)*. Briefly, this division speaks of the sacrificial cult and the sanctuary in which the cult is conducted. The law pays special attention to the matter of the status of the property of the altar and of the sanctuary, both utilized in the actual sacrificial rites, and property whose value supports the cult and sanctuary in general. All of these are deemed to be sanctified, that is, they are "holy things."

The Division of Purities presents a very simple system of three parts: sources of uncleanness, objects and substances susceptible to uncleanness, and modes of purification from uncleanness. This division tells the story of what makes a particular object unclean and what makes it clean. The tractates on these several topics are: 1. sources of uncleanness – *Ohalot, Negaim, Niddah, Makhshirin, Zabim, Tebul Yom*; 2. objects and substances susceptible to uncleanness – *Kelim, Tohorot, Uqsin*; and 3. modes of purification – *Parah, Miqvaot, Yadayim*. Viewed as a whole, the Division of Purities treats the interplay of persons, food, and liquids. Dry inanimate objects or food are not susceptible to uncleanness. What is wet is susceptible. So liquids activate the system. What is unclean, moreover, emerges from uncleanness through the operation of liquids, specifically, through immersion in fit water of requisite volume and in natural condition. Liquids thus deactivate the system. Water in its natural condition is what concludes the process by removing uncleanness. Water in its unnatural condition, that is, deliberately affected by human agency, is what imparts susceptibility to uncleanness. The uncleanness of persons, furthermore, is signified by body liquids or flux in the case of the menstruating woman (Niddah) and the *zab* (Zabim).Corpse uncleanness is conceived to be a kind of effluent, a viscous gas, which flows like liquid. Utensils receive uncleanness when they form receptacles able to contain liquid. In sum, we have here a system in which the invisible flow of fluid-like substances or powers serves to put food, drink, and receptacles into the status of uncleanness and to remove those things from that status. Whether or not we call the system "metaphysical," it certainly has no material base but is conditioned upon highly abstract notions. Thus in material terms, the effect of liquid is upon food, drink, utensils, and humans. The consequence has to do with who may eat and drink what food and liquid, and what food and drink may be consumed in which pots and pans. These loci are specified by tractates on utensils (*Kelim*) and on food and drink (*Tohorot* and *Uqsin*).

With this topical survey in mind, let us return to the crisis precipitated by the destruction of the Second Temple. To the founders of the Mishnah, the aftermath of the first defeat brought an end to the orderly life of the villages and the land and to the reliable relationship of calendar and crop with cult – all joined to the movement of moon, sun, and fixed stars. The problematic of the age therefore was located in that middle range of life between the personal tragedy of individuals, who live and die, and the national catastrophe of the history of Israel. That accounts for the frame of reference of the Mishnah and the language that its authorship has employed. The Pentateuchal Torah is narrative and presents law in concrete terms. The Mishnah's Torah is general and speaks in descriptive, present-tense language. It does not speak of special occasions or events, as does the Pentateuch, but in very general terms.

With no cult, no officiating priesthood, no Temple, no Jerusalem, the Torah now had to speak of that other realm of the sacred, the home and village, the field and family. That explains why the Mishnah talks of pots and pans, of menstruation and dead creeping things, of ordinary water which, because of the circumstance of its collection and location, possesses extraordinary power; of the commonplace corpse and ubiquitous diseased person; of genitalia and excrement, toilet seats and the flux of penises, of stems of pomegranates and stalks of leeks; of rain and earth and wood, metal, glass, and hide. This language is filled with words for neutral things of humble existence. It does not speak of holy things and is not symbolic in its substance. All things must be in order, for all things will then be hallowed by God who orders all things. So said the priests' creation-tale.

Beyond the catastrophe of 70 CE and the calamity of 132–135, the Mishnah came into being to reaffirm, within the oral Torah, the principal message of the written Torah: Israel, the people, is holy to God. But in order to restate that message, the framers of the Mishnah had to add a document to the Torah, and, in doing so, they replicated the program of Ezra who, to speak of God and Israel, wrote the Torah.

— 5 —

The Formation of the Dual Torah:
The Yerushalmi and Israel's Sanctification Now
and Salvation in the End

The fourth century marks the first century of Western civilization. The West as we have known it from Constantine to the nineteenth century carried forward three principal elements of the heritage of antiquity and made of them one. These were 1. Roman law and institutions; 2. the legacy of ancient Israel, the Hebrew Scriptures; and 3. Christianity as religion of the state and formative force in culture. The West was what it was because of Christianity. So the history of the West began when Christianity attained that position in politics and culture that it was to occupy for the history of the West, until nearly the present day. And, as a matter of fact, the Judaism of the dual Torah then reached that fundamental formulation that would characterize that system through the rest of history, to the present: the joining of sanctification in the here and the now to salvation at the end of time, the stress on the dual media of the Torah, with the sages or rabbis' writings forming part of God's revelation to our rabbi, Moses, at Sinai. No document that reached closure prior to the end of the fourth century expressed these fundamental positions. But everything would be in place in the documents that reached closure at the end of the fourth century.

The literary expansion of the Torah is readily traced. The oral Torah beyond the Mishnah addressed two documents, the Mishnah and Scripture. The explanations of the Mishnah begin with the Tosefta, a corpus of supplementary sayings, and continue with the Talmud of the Land of Israel, ca. 400 CE, a systematic exegesis of the Mishnah, and the Talmud of Babylonia, also a systematic explanation of the Mishnah, ca. 500–600 CE. A separate body of exegesis, to which we turn in chapter 6, concentrates on Scripture first of all, particularly books of the Pentateuch or Five Books attributed to Moses. These compilations called Midrash (plural, Midrashim), meaning exegeses of Scripture, have to be placed into context, even though it is only in the next chapter that we shall consider what they contribute to the unfolding of the Torah. The compilations include Genesis Rabbah, on the book of Genesis, commonly regarded as a work of ca. 400 CE; Leviticus Rabbah, on the book of Leviticus, ordinarily dated about 450 CE; and works on legal passages of Exodus, Leviticus, Numbers, and Deuteronomy: Sifra, on Leviticus, Sifré Numbers, and Sifré Deuteronomy. These latter are of indeterminate date, but probably of the later third or fourth century. There were various other writings of the same age, for instance, Pesiqta deRav Kahana, a collection of exegeses of verses of Scripture important on special occasions, following the style and conceptual program of Leviticus Rabbah; The Fathers according to Rabbi Nathan, an amplification of the Mishnah-tractate; The Fathers, in which stories about sages are told to enrich the Mishnah-tractate's account of sayings assigned to sages. All together these and related contemporary writings constitute "the oral Torah" as it had reached writing by the end of late antiquity, signified by the Muslim conquest of the Christian Middle East. It is, in writing, that body of tradition assigned to the authority of God's revelation to Moses at Mount Sinai.

Accordingly, the oral Torah reached written form in two stages: the one marked in about 200 CE by the framing of the Mishnah and its closely associated documents, the Tosefta and tractate Avot; the other defined in about 400 CE by the exegesis of the Mishnah and of Scripture in the Talmud of the Land of Israel and its friends, Genesis Rabbah and Leviticus Rabbah, respectively. It is to this second phase that we turn when we address the Talmud of the Land of Israel.

What happened beyond 200 and before 400? Two processes occurred, one of which generated the other. The first of the two was that the Mishnah was extensively stated, line by line, word by word. The modes of study were mainly three. First, the sages asked about the meanings of words and phrases. Second, they worked on the comparison of one set of laws with another, finding the underlying principles of each and comparing and harmonizing those principles. So they formed a tight and large fabric of the rather episodic rules.

Third, they moved beyond the narrow limits of the Mishnah into still broader and more speculative areas of thought.

So, in all, the sages responsible for administering the law also expounded and, willy nilly, expanded the law. Ultimately, in both countries, the work of Mishnah-commentary developed into two large-scale documents, each called a Talmud. We have them as the Talmud of the Land of Israel (which I have translated into English), completed by about 400, and the Talmud of Babylonia, completed by about 600. In both of these documents, sages vastly articulated the theme of the Mishnah, the sanctification of Israel. But what of salvation? Where, when, and how did sages then shaping Judaism address that other and complementary category of Israel's existence? And, we further ask, is the work of linking the Mishnah to Scripture the only kind of scriptural commentary sages produced between the first and the fourth century? Not at all. Sages turned to Scripture to seek the laws of Israel's history, to ask the questions of salvation, of Israel's relationship to God that, in the Mishnah and in the works of amplification of the Mishnah, they tended to neglect. When did they do so?

The answer to that question brings us to the expansion of the Torah in the fourth century. That is when the sages produced the great works on Genesis, in Genesis Rabbah, and on Leviticus, in Leviticus Rabbah, which answered the questions of salvation, of the meaning and end of Israel's history, that the Mishnah and its continuator-writings did not take up. Why in the fourth century in particular? Because, as I shall explain, the historical crisis precipitated by Christianity's takeover of the Roman Empire and its government demanded answers from Israel's sages: What does it mean? What does history mean? Where are we to find guidance to the meaning of our past – and our future? Sages looked, then, to Genesis, maintaining that the story of the creation of the world and the beginning of Israel would show the way toward the meaning of history and the salvation of Israel.

They further looked to Leviticus, and in Leviticus Rabbah they accomplished the link between the sanctification of Israel through its cult and priesthood, which is the theme of the book of Leviticus, and the salvation of Israel, which is the concern of the commentators to that book. What they did was to place Israel, the people, at the center of the story of Leviticus, applying to the life of the people of

Israel those rules of sanctification that, when observed, would prepare Israel, holy Israel, for salvation. So, in a nutshell, the framers of Leviticus Rabbah imparted to the book of Leviticus the message, in response to the destruction of the Temple, that the authors of the Mishnah had addressed two hundred years earlier: Israel's holiness endures. Sanctifying the life of Israel now will lead to the salvation of Israel in time to come. Sanctification and salvation, the natural world and the supernatural, the rules of society and the rules of history, all become one in the life of Israel.

So the dual Torah followed a linear and unitary development, from stage to stage, yielding a harmonious and cogent system. The principal question formulated by the sages, who after 70 produced the Mishnah, centered upon the sanctification of Israel now that the Temple, the locus of holiness, lay in ruins and the cult was no more. But that central concern ignored a second fundamental consideration in Israel's life, and that was the issue of salvation. For while the framers of the first document of the oral Torah described a steady-state world, that is not how Israel, the holy people, in the land of Israel, experienced the everyday. Quite to the contrary, times changed, important historical events affected the life of Israel in its land, and the pretense that the status of equilibrium in the condition of holiness could be attained contradicted perceived reality. That is why the Judaism of the dual Torah would ultimately set forth a twin-ideal: sanctification of the everyday life in the here and now which, when fully realized, would lead to salvation of all Israel in the age to come.

Now that we have accounted for the redefinition of the bounds of the sacred from Temple and cult to the life of the people in its land, how shall we explain the reshaping of the system as a whole to encompass not only sanctification but salvation as well? And why was the issue of salvation transformed from a chronic concern to an acute and critical problem? The answers to those questions brings us to the pages of the Talmud of the Land of Israel, a massive document that sets forth in the form of a sustained commentary to thirty-nine of the Mishnah's sixty-two tractates a system that is essentially a-symmetrical to the Mishnah. The Talmud of the Land of Israel cites and glosses the Mishnah, at the same time including in its pages materials quite independent of the Mishnah's.

Brought to closure at about 400 CE, the Talmud of the land of

Israel came into existence nearly a century after a political cataclysm as far-reaching in its implications as the destruction of the Temple in Jerusalem and the end of the Jews' existence as an autonomous state within the Roman imperial system. What happened was that in 312 the Roman empire, through Emperor Constantine, declared Christianity to be a legal religion, and within the next fifty years Christianity became the religion of the Roman empire. A series of Christian emperors accorded to Christianity political predominance, such as its founders and framers cannot have imagined for themselves. When, moreover, in 361 Emperor Julian reverted to paganism and also permitted the Jews to commence rebuilding the Temple in Jerusalem, the emperor was killed in a war against Iran and the Christian emperors in the succession thereafter pointed to that fact as proof of God's favor for the Christian state. The Christians were quick to point out to Israel in the land of Israel that this astounding turn of events vindicated their faith and, furthermore, disproved the Jews' claim that salvation, in fulfillment of the promises of the prophets, lay in the future. To the contrary, they said, the salvation for Israel of which the prophets spoke took place long ago, in the time of the return to Zion in Ezra's day, and the sole salvation awaiting Israel lay with conversion to Christianity.

The shift from pagan to Christian Rome took place in the fourth century, from the initial moment at which Constantine accorded to Christianity the status of licit and favored religion at the outset and by the end the official and governing religion of the state. Judaism and Christianity in late antiquity, we realize, present histories that mirror one another. When Christianity began in the first century, Judaism was the dominant tradition in the Holy Land and framed its ideas within a political framework until the early fifth century. Christianity there was subordinate and had to work out against the background of a politically definitive Judaism. From the fourth century, the time of Constantine onward, matters reversed themselves. Now Christianity predominated, expressing its ideas in political and institutional terms. Judaism, by contrast, had lost its political foundations and faced the task of working out its self-understanding in terms of a world defined by Christianity, now everywhere triumphant and in charge of politics. The important shift came in the early fourth century, the West's first century. That was when the West began in the union of Christian religion and Roman rule. It also was when the Judaism that thrived in the West reached the definition it was to exhibit for the next fifteen centuries until, as I shall note at the end, our own time.

The importance of the age of Constantine in the history of Judaism derives from a simple fact. It was at this time that important Judaic documents undertook to deal with agenda defined, for both Judaism and Christianity, by the triumph of Christianity. Important Christian thinkers reflected on issues presented by the political revolution in the status of Christianity. Issues of the rewriting of human history, the canonization of the Bible as the Old and New Testaments, the restatement of the challenge and claim of Christ the King as Messiah against the continuing "unbelief" of Israel (phrased from the Christian viewpoint, Jews would refer to their continuing belief in God's power to save the world at the end of time), the definition of who is Israel – these make their appearance in Christian writings of the day. And these issues derive from the common agenda of both Judaism and Christianity, namely, the Holy Scriptures of ancient Israel, received in Judaism as the written half of the one whole Torah of Moses, our Rabbi, and in Christianity as the Old Testament.

What in fact did the sages of the fourth century documents, in particular, the Talmud of the Land of Israel, have to say to Israel? They turned back to Scripture, rereading the two books that mattered, 1. the one on the creation of the world and of the children of Israel (Genesis), and 2. the one on the sanctification of Israel. So they proposed to explain history by rereading the book of Genesis. There they found the lesson that what happened to the patriarchs in the beginning signals what would happen to their children later on. And Jacob then is Israel now, just as Esau then is Rome now. Israel remains Israel, bearer of the blessing. They explain the status and authority of the traditions – now two hundred years old – of the Mishnah and related writings by assigning to them a place in the Torah. Specifically, in the canonical documents of the period at hand we for the first time find clear reference to the notion that when God revealed the Torah to Moses at Sinai, part of the Torah was in the medium of writing, the other part in the medium of memory, hence oral.

And, it would later be explained, the Mishnah and much else enjoyed the status of oral Torah. They explain the messiah-claim of Israel in very simple terms. Israel indeed will receive the messiah, but salvation at the end of time awaits the sanctification of Israel in the here and now. That will take place through humble and obedient loyalty to the Torah. They counter the claim that there is a new Israel in place of the old, and this they do by rereading the book of Leviticus, with its message of sanctification of Israel, finding in that book a typology of the great empires – Babylonia, Media, Greece, Rome. The coming fifth and final sovereign will be Israel's messiah. So, in all, the points important to Christianity in the advent of Constantine and the Christian empire – history vindicates Christ, the New Testament explains the Old, the Messiah has come and his claim has now been proved truthful, and the old Israel is done for and will not have a messiah in the future – all those points were countered for the Jews in a self-evidently valid manner by the writings of the fourth-century sages.

The rabbinic system, which laid stress on the priority of salvation over sanctification, on the dual media by which the Torah came forth from Sinai, on the messianic dimension of Israel's everyday life, and on the permanence of Israel's position as God's first love – came to first articulate expression in the Talmud of the Land of Israel and related writings – there, and not in the Mishnah and in its companions. The reason for this is clear: the system responded to a competing system, one heir of the ancient Israelite Scripture answering another heir and its claims. The siblings would struggle, like Esau and Jacob, for the common blessing. For the Jewish people, in any event, the system of the fourth-century sages would endure for millennia as self-evidently right and persuasive.

The questions at hand – the meaning of history, the identification of the messiah, the definition of Israel, God's people – dominated because they framed in theological terms the political crisis under way through the century, with the shock of Christian success followed by the despair of the failure of Julian's scheme to rebuild the Temple. That explains why the shape of Judaism, as laid forth in documents redacted in the fourth and early fifth century, exhibits remarkable congruence to the contours of the same intellectual program. Specifically, in the Judaism of the sages of the land of Israel who redacted the principal documents at hand, were both a doctrine and an apologetic remarkably relevant to the issues presented to both Christianity and Judaism by the crisis of Christianity's worldly triumph.

Jews and Christians alike believed in the Israelite Scriptures and thus understood that major turnings in history carried a message from God. That message bore meaning for questions of salvation and the messiah, the identification of God's will in Scripture, the determination of who is Israel and what it means to be Israel, and similar questions of a profoundly historical and social character. So it is no wonder that the enormous turning represented by the advent of a Christian empire should have precipitated deep thought on these issues, important as they are in the fourth-century thought of both Judaic sages and Christian theologians. The specification of the message at hand would, of course, produce long-term differences between the Christianity and the Judaism of the time as well.

The success of the Judaism shaped in this place, in this time, is clear. Refined and vastly restated in the Talmud of Babylonia two hundred years later, the system of Judaism worked out here and now enjoyed the status of self-evidence among Jews confronted with Christian governments and Christian populations over the next fifteen hundred years. So far as ideas matter in bonding a group, the success among the people of Israel in Europe, west and east alike, of the Judaism defined in the fourth-century writings of the sages of the land of Israel, derives from the power and persuasive effect of the ideas of that Judaism. Coming to the surface in the writings of the age, particularly the Talmud of the land of Israel, Genesis Rabbah, and Leviticus Rabbah, that Judaism therefore secured for despairing Israel a long future of hope and confident endurance.

Prior to the time of Constantine, the documents of Judaism that evidently reached closure – the Mishnah, tractate Abot, the Tosefta – scarcely took cognizance of Christianity and did not deem the new faith to be much of a challenge. If the scarce and scattered allusions do mean to refer to Christianity at all, then sages regarded it as an irritant, an exasperating heresy among Jews who should have known better. But, then, neither Jews nor pagans took much interest in Christianity in the new faith's first century and a half. The authors of the Mishnah framed a system to which Christianity bore no relevance whatsoever; theirs were problems presented in an altogether different context. For their part, pagan writers were indifferent to Christianity, not mentioning it until about 160. Only when Christian evangelism enjoyed some solid success toward the later part of that century did pagans compose apologetic works attacking Christianity. Celsus stands at the start, followed by Porphyry in the third century. But by the fourth century, pagans and Jews alike knew that they faced a formidable, powerful enemy. Pagan writings speak explicitly and accessibly. The answers sages worked out for the intellectual challenge of the hour do not emerge equally explicitly and accessibly. But they are there, and when we ask the right questions and establish the context of discourse, we hear the answers in the Talmud of the Land of Israel, Genesis Rabbah, and Leviticus Rabbah, as clearly as we hear pagans' answers in the writings of Porphyry and Julian, not to mention the Christians' answers in the rich and diverse writings of the fourth-century fathers, such as Eusebius, Jerome, John Chrysostom, and Aphrahat, to mention just four.

The Judaism of the sages of the Land of Israel who redacted the principal documents at hand therefore framed both a doctrine and an apologetic remarkably relevant to the issues presented to both Christianity and Judaism by the crisis of Christianity's worldly triumph. Why the common set of questions? Because, as I said, Jews and Christians alike believed in the Israelite Scriptures, and so understood that major turnings in history carried a message from God. The specification of the message at hand, of course, would produce long-term differences between the Christianity and the Judaism of the time as well. But the shared program brought the two religions into protracted confrontation on an intersecting set of questions. The struggle between the one and the other – a struggle that would continue until our own time – originated in the simple fact that, to begin with, both religions agreed on pretty much everything that mattered.

They differed on little and therefore made much of that little. Scripture taught them both that vast changes in the affairs of empires came about because of God's will. History proved principles of theology. In that same Torah prophets promised the coming of the messiah, who would bring salvation. Who was, and is, that messiah, and how shall we know? And that same Torah addressed a particular people, Israel, promising that people the expression of God's favor and love. But who is Israel, and who is not Israel? So Scripture defined the categories that were shared in common. Scripture filled those categories with deep meaning. That is why to begin with a kind of dialogue – made up, to be sure, of two monologues on the same topics – could commence. The dialogue continued for centuries because the conditions that to begin with precipitated it, specifically the rise to political dominance of Christianity and the subordination of Judaism, remained constant for fifteen hundred years.

The oral Torah – now the Talmud of the Land of Israel and closely related writings – stated in the circumstance and language of crisis the message of Sinai that, in written form, had come down from ancient times. Just as the exodus from Egypt and the revelation given to Moses precipitated a vast effort to write down and preserve the truth of that moment in the language and categories of that setting, so the events of late antiquity for Israel, the Jewish people, precipitated a vast and enduring work of preserving the revealed truth of the hour in the language and categories of that hour. The ancient rabbis looked out upon a world destroyed and still smoking in the aftermath of calamity, but they spoke of rebirth and renewal. The holy Temple lay in ruins, but they asked about sanctification. The old history was over, but they looked toward future history.

For their purposes the sages of this age and its writings appealed to the truth of the written Torah, but they also wrote down and preserved as Torah from Sinai the truth their own day had received. The task of holding together sanctification in the here and now and salvation at the end of time, the enormous challenge of finding warrant in the written Torah for the truth revealed in the oral Torah – these two challenges produced the response before us: the vast canon of the oral Torah worked out in relationship to the written one. Theirs is a message that what is true and real is the opposite of what people perceive. God stands for paradox. Strength comes through weakness, salvation through acceptance and obedience, sanctification through the ordinary and profane, which can be made holy. Israel's condition testifies to the deeper truth, the real structure of human life: sanctification outside of a temple, life out of the grave, eternity from death – all these paradoxes corresponded to the simple social fact that holy and supernatural Israel lived out its days as a conquered and subordinated people among other peoples. So, we may say, social reality in the imagination of sages pointed to the deeper truth, for the deeper the truth, the richer the paradox! Israel's present condition presents a paradox and, out of reflection on the social realities concealed by contemporary politics (as sages would have understood matters), sages penetrated into those revealed mysteries of the Torah – their Torah, the oral part – that would sustain Israel from then to now.

So the Judaism of the dual Torah as a matter of fact so successfully addressed the condition of Israel, the holy people, that its Judaism predominated from late antiquity to our own day. The reason lay in its success in answering the two urgent questions made critical by the political changes in the Jews' condition: their loss of standing as a political entity on the one side, and the triumph of Christianity in the Roman empire on the other. The Jews' condition, defined by Christianity, affirmed later on by Islam, was that of subordination and, at best, toleration. For long centuries afterward, the Jews' Judaism drew upon the writings of the period at hand to address the now-chronic issues of political subordination and religious disappointment and resentment. Only when the world in which Jews lived found its definitions other than in Christianity, and the Jews' political circumstances were vastly changed from the ones that prevailed until the formation of the nation-state within the capitalist world, did new Judaisms emerge, each asking its urgent question and offering its self-evidently valid answer.

That explains the importance of the Talmud of the Land of Israel as a commentary to and successor and heir of the Mishnah. The urgent question that predominates in that enormous document, which is given the form of an extended elaboration of the Mishnah, is the issue of salvation: when, why, and above all, how long postponed? In answering these questions, the authors of the Talmud of the Land of Israel completed the forming of the symbolic system of the Judaism of the dual Torah. For it is only in the Talmud of the land of Israel and its closely allied documents, Genesis Rabbah and Leviticus Rabbah, about 400–450 CE, that that Judaism's principal and indicative doctrines, symbols, and beliefs came to full and complete expression.

It remains to ask how precisely the Talmud of the Land of Israel treats the Mishnah, and in what way this Talmud treats the Mishnah in relationship to the written Scriptures in particular. It is at just this time that the doctrine of the dual Torah, oral and written, first comes to explicit expression. In the following passage of the Talmud of the Land of Israel, we find the theory that there is a tradition separate from and in addition to the written Torah. This tradition it knows as "the teachings of scribes." The Mishnah is not identified as the collection of those teachings.

III. A. Associates in the name of R. Yohanan: "The words of scribes are more beloved than the words of Torah and more cherished than words of Torah: 'Your palate is like the best wine' (Song 7:9)."

B. Simeon bar Ba in the name of R. Yohanan: "The words of scribes are more beloved than the words of Torah and more cherished than words of Torah: 'For your love is better than wine' (Song 1:2)." . . .

D. R. Ishmael repeated the following: "The words of Torah are subject to prohibition, and they are subject to remission; they are subject to lenient rulings, and they are subject to strict rulings. But words of scribes all are subject only to strict interpretation, for we have learned there: He who rules, 'There is no requirement to wear phylacteries,' in order to transgress the teachings of the Torah, is exempt. But if he said, 'There are five partitions in the phylactery, instead of four,' in order to add to what the scribes have taught, he is liable [M. San. 11:3]."

E. R. Haninah in the name of R. Idi in the name of R. Tanhum b. R. Hiyya: "More stringent are the words of the elders than the words of the prophets. For it is written, 'Do not preach' – thus they preach – 'one should not preach of such things' (Micah 2:6). And it is written, "[If a man should go about and utter wind and lies, saying,] 'I will preach to you of wine and strong drink,' he would be the preacher for this people!" (Micah 2:11).

F. "A prophet and an elder – to what are they comparable? To a king who sent two senators of his to a certain province. Concerning one of them he wrote, 'If he does not show you my seal and signet, do not believe him.' But concerning the other one he wrote, 'Even though he does not show you my seal and signet, believe him.' So in the case of the prophet, he has had to write, 'If a prophet arises among you . . . and gives you a sign or a wonder . . . (Deut. 13:1). But here [with regard to an elder:] . . . according to the instructions which they give you . . . ' (Deut. 17:11) [without a sign or a wonder]."

Talmud of the Land of Israel Tractate Abodah Zarah 2:7

What is important in the foregoing anthology is the distinction between teachings contained in the Torah and teachings in the name or authority of "scribes." These latter teachings are associated with quite specific details of the law and are indicated in the Mishnah's rule itself. Further, at E we have "elders" (that is, sages) as against prophets. What happens to the Mishnah in the Talmud of the Land of Israel shows us how the Talmud's founders viewed the Mishnah.

That view may be stated very simply. The Mishnah rarely cites verses of Scripture in support of its propositions. The Talmud routinely adduces Scriptural bases for the Mishnah's laws. The Mishnah seldom undertakes the exegesis of verses of Scripture for any purpose. The Talmud consistently investigates the meaning of verses of Scripture and does so for a variety of purposes. Accordingly, the Talmud, subordinate as it is to the Mishnah, regards the Mishnah as subordinate to and contingent upon Scripture. That is why, in the Talmud's view, the Mishnah requires the support of prooftexts of Scripture. Let me state the upshot with the necessary emphasis: that fact can mean only that, by itself, the Mishnah exercises no autonomous authority and enjoys no independent standing or norm-setting status. This other half of the one whole Torah, the oral half, is subordinate; but it also is part of the Torah.

A broad shift was taking place in the generations that received the Mishnah, that is, over the third and fourth centuries. If the sages of the second century, who made the Mishnah as we know it, spoke in their own name and in the name of the logic of their own minds, those who followed, certainly the ones who flourished in the later fourth century, took a quite different view. Reverting to ancient authority like others of the age, they turned back to Scripture, deeming it the source of certainty about truth. Unlike their masters in the Mishnah, theirs was a quest for a higher authority than the logic of their own minds. The shift from age to age then is clear. The second-century masters took commonplaces of Scripture, well-known facts, and stated them wholly in their own language and context. Fourth-century masters phrased commonplaces of the Mishnah or banalities of worldly wisdom, so far as they could, in the language of Scripture and its context.

The real issue turns out to have been not the Mishnah at all, not even its diverse sayings vindicated one by one. What a sage says is made to refer to Scripture for proof; it must follow that, in the natural course of things, a rule of the Mishnah and of the Tosefta will likewise be asked to refer also to Scripture. The fact that the living sage validates what he says through Scripture explains why the sage also validates through verses of Scripture what the ancient sages of the Mishnah and Tosefta say. It is one undivided phenomenon. The reception of the Mishnah constitutes merely one massive testimony to a prevalent attitude of mind, important for the age of the Talmud of the Land of Israel, the third and fourth centuries, not solely for the Mishnah. The stated issue was the standing of the Mishnah. But the heart of the matter turns out to have been the authority of the sage himself, who identified with the authors of the Mishnah and claimed authoritatively to interpret the Mishnah and much else, specifically including Scripture. So the appeal to Scripture in behalf of the Mishnah represents simply one more expression of what proved critical in the formative age of Judaism: the person of the holy man himself, this new man, this incarnate Torah. When revelation – Torah – became flesh, Judaism was born.

The result for the history of Judaism may be stated very briefly. The history of Judaism then proceeded in three stages: the written Torah, defining the basic issues of Israel's life; then the Mishnah, contributing to the dual Torah the revision of the theory of Israel's sanctification in response to the destruction of the Second Temple; and third, the Talmud of the Land of Israel and related writings, adding to the complete account of Israel's supernatural life the reaffirmation of salvation in response to the advent of triumphant Christianity. These second and third phases in the formation of the one whole Torah show us, in the Mishnah, a version of the Judaism of the dual Torah that reached writing before Christianity made an impact on the Judaic sages, while the Talmud and its associates show us the changes that were made in the encounter with Christianity as the triumphant religion of the Roman state. The Judaism that took shape in the Land of Israel in the fourth century, attested by documents brought to closure in the fifth, responded to that Christianity and in particular to its challenge to the Israel of that place and time and flourished, in Israel, the Jewish people, so long as the West was Christian. That, sum and substance, is the story of the most important Judaic system of all times.

What shifted in the Talmud of the Land of Israel's transformation of the received system was its theologians' redefinition of salvation from the here and now to the end of time. And that change, of course, was not only plausible; it also was necessary in light of the catastrophe at hand. The reason for the transfer of the hope for salvation from now to the end of time derives from a political event in some ways bearing greater weight than the destruction of the Temple in 70. It is the success of the competing and rival version of the written Torah, Christianity, with its fully articulated Bible, made up of the Old Testament and the New Testament, with its claim to succeed and replace the old Israel, with its proof for the kingship of Jesus as Christ in the Christian empire, and with its dismissal of Israel after the flesh as now rejected and set aside by God.

With the triumph of Christianity through Constantine and his successors in the West, Christianity's explicit claims, now validated in world-shaking events of the age, demanded a reply. The sages of the Talmud provided it. At those very specific points at which the Christian challenge met old Israel's world-view head-on, sages' doctrines responded. What did Israel's sages have to present as the Torah's answer to the cross? It was the Torah. This took three forms. The Torah was defined in the doctrine, first of the status as oral and memorized revelation of the Mishnah and, by implication, of other rabbinical writings. The Torah, moreover, was presented as the encompassing symbol of Israel's salvation. The Torah, finally, was embodied in the person of the messiah who, of course, would be a rabbi. The Torah in all three modes confronted the cross with its doctrine of the triumphant Christ, Messiah and king, ruler now of earth as of heaven. That is why the dual Torah formed the generative symbol for the Judaism that triumphed; it dealt with the urgent and critical question that had to be confronted, and it provided an answer that, to believers, was self-evidently valid, necessary, and sufficient.

6

The Hebrew Scriptures in the Dual Torah:
Midrash

Exegesis of the Hebrew Scriptures was made necessary to begin with because of the character of the Mishnah as the initial document of the dual Torah. That exegesis bears the title "Midrash." The word Midrash is used in three ways. First, Midrash refers to the processes of scriptural exegesis carried on by diverse groups of Jews from the time of ancient Israel to nearly the present day. It is difficult to specify what the word Midrash in Hebrew expresses that the word exegesis in English does not. The word Midrash further stands for a compilation of scriptural exegeses, as in "that Midrash deals with the Book of Joshua." Midrash here refers to a compilation of exegeses; hence the statement means, "That compilation of exegeses deals with the Book of Joshua." Compilation or composite, in the present context, clearly serves more accurately to convey meaning than Midrash.

Finally, the word Midrash stands for the written composition (for example, a paragraph with a beginning, middle, and end in which a completed thought is laid forth) resulting from the process of Midrash. In this setting "a Midrash" refers to a paragraph or a unit of exegetical exposition in which a verse of the Hebrew Scriptures is subjected to some form of exegesis or other. In this usage one may say, "Let me now cite the Midrash," meaning a particular passage of exegesis, a paragraph or other completed whole unit of exegetical thought, a composition that provides an exegesis of a particular verse. I use the word composition in this sense. Since the authors of the Mishnah only rarely cite prooftexts for positions that they reach, it was necessary for their heirs to relate their results to the written Torah. That explains why the first task of the Midrash-compilations, in drawing attention back to Scripture, was to answer: What is the relationship between the Mishnah and the established Scripture of Israel, the written Torah?

The Mishnah only occasionally adduces texts of the Scriptures in support of its rules. Its framers worked out their own topical program, only part of which intersects with that of the laws of the Pentateuch. They followed their own principles of organization and development. They wrote in their own kind of Hebrew, which is quite different from biblical Hebrew. So the question naturally arose, Can we through sheer logic discover the law? Or must we tease laws out of Scripture through commentary, through legal exegesis? The Mishnah represented an extreme in this debate, since so many of its topics do not derive from Scripture and, further, a large part of its laws ignore Scripture's pertinent texts (these texts are simply not cited). When, moreover, the framers of the Sayings of the Fathers, whom we have already met, placed sages named in the Mishnah on the list of those who stand within the chain of tradition beginning at Sinai, they did not assign to those sages verses of Scripture, the written Torah (except in one or two instances). Rather, the Torah-saying assigned to each of the named sages is not scriptural at all. So the sages enjoy an independent standing and authority on their own; they are not subordinate to Scripture and their sayings enjoy equal standing with sentences of Scripture.

The work of exegesis of the Mishnah therefore drew attention also to the relationship of the Mishnah to Scripture. Consequently, important works of biblical commentary emerged in the third and fourth centuries. In these works, focused on such books as Leviticus (Sifra), Numbers (Sifré to Numbers) and Deuteronomy (Sifré to Deuteronomy), a paramount issue is whether law emerges solely on the basis of processes of reasoning, or whether only through looking in verses of Scripture can we uncover solid basis for the rules of the Mishnah. In that discourse we find the citation of a verse of Scripture followed by a verbatim citation of a passage of the Mishnah. Since this mode of reading Scripture is not apt to be familiar to many readers, I will give a concrete example of how the process of Mishnah-exegesis in relationship to Scripture-exegesis was carried forward in the third and fourth centuries. The following is from Sifré to Numbers:

A. " . . . every man's holy thing shall be his; whatever any man gives to the priest shall be his" (Num. 5:10).

B. On the basis of this statement you draw the following rule:

C. If a priest on his own account makes a sacrificial offering, even though it falls into the week [during which] another priestly watch than his own [is in charge of the actual cult, making the offerings and receiving the dues], lo, that priest owns the priestly portions of the offering, and the right of offering it up belongs to him [and not to the priest ordinarily on duty at that time, who otherwise would retain the rights to certain portions of the animal] [T. Men. 13:17].

Sifré to Numbers Pisqa VI:II.1

What we see is simply a citation of the verse plus a law in a prior writing (in this case not the Mishnah, but the Tosefta, a compilation of supplements to the Mishnah's laws) which the verse is supposed to sustain. The formal traits require 1. citation of a verse, with or without comment, followed by 2. verbatim citation of a passage of the Mishnah or the Tosefta. The result is a formal construction in which we simply juxtapose a verse, without or with intervening words of explanation, with a passage of the Mishnah (or the Tosefta). When sages proposed to provide for Scripture a counterpart, a commentary, to what they were even then creating for the Mishnah, they sought to build bridges from the Mishnah to Scripture. Three systematic exegeses of books of Scripture or the written Torah investigated the relationship between Scripture and the Mishnah: Sifra to Leviticus, Sifré to Numbers, and another Sifré to Deuteronomy.[1]

Other Midrash-compilations on the written Torah which we have already met include Genesis Rabbah, a reading of the book of Genesis to interpret the history and salvation of Israel today in light of the history and salvation of the patriarchs and matriarchs of old, deemed to form the founders of the family of Israel after the flesh. A second important work, assigned to about the next half-century, Leviticus Rabbah, about 450 CE, read for the lessons of Israel's salvation the

---

[1] Considerable interest in the same question is shown by authors in the Tosefta, the Talmud of the Land of Israel, and the Talmud of Babylonia, which we shall meet in the next chapter.

book of Leviticus, which stresses issues of the sanctification of Israel. So Leviticus was reread for its lessons regarding how Israel's sanctification in the here and now led to Israel's salvation at the end of time. Alongside were other treatments of biblical books important in synagogue liturgy, particularly the scrolls of hagiography that enjoyed prominence in synagogue liturgy: Lamentations, Esther, Ruth, Song of Songs, treated by Lamentations Rabbati, Esther Rabbah, Ruth Rabbah, and Song of Songs Rabbah respectively. A remarkable compilation of scriptural lessons pertinent to the special occasions of the synagogue, Pesiqta deRab Kahana, reached closure at the same time – the fifth or sixth centuries – as well.

Can we characterize the modes of reading the written Torah in these components of the oral Torah? Midrash-hermeneutics, that is, approaches to the systematic interpretation of Scripture, yielded three kinds of readings of the written Torah in the oral: Midrash-as-paraphrase, Midrash-as-prophecy, and Midrash-as-parable or allegorical reading of Scripture.

In the first of these, the exegete would paraphrase Scripture, imposing fresh meanings by the word-choices or even by adding additional phrases or sentences, thus revising the meaning of the received text. I call this Midrash-as-paraphrase because the fresh meaning is imputed by obliterating the character of the original text and rendering or translating it in a new sense. The barrier between the text and the comment is obscured, and the commentator joins in the composing of the text. Midrash-as-paraphrase may also include fresh materials, but these are presented as if they formed an integral part of the original text. In the other two modes of Midrash, the boundary between text and imputed meaning is always clearly marked. Sifra and the two Sifrés operate along these lines.

In the second, the exegete would ask Scripture to explain meanings of events near at hand, and Scripture would serve as a means of prophetic reading of the contemporary world. Midrash-as-prophecy produces the identification of a biblical statement or event with a contemporary happening. Here the scriptural verse or text retains its particularity, being kept distinct from the commentary or exegesis. In its substance, however, as against its form, Midrash-as-prophecy treats the historical life of ancient Israel and the contemporary times of the exegete as essentially the same, reading the former as a prefiguring of the latter. Through Midrash-as-prophecy, therefore,

Scripture addresses contemporary times as a guide to what is happening even now and, more to the point, what is going to happen in the near future. We already realize that Genesis Rabbah and Leviticus Rabbah work on the problems of history.

In the third type of Midrash-as-process, which for the sake of convenience I call Midrash-as-parable, though the categories of allegory or metaphor also pertain, the exegete reads Scripture in terms other than those in which the scriptural writer speaks. Scripture, for instance, may tell the story of love of man and woman in the Song of Songs, but Judaic and Christian exegetes heard the song of the love of God and Israel or God and the church. Scripture in Genesis speaks of the family of Abraham, Isaac, and Jacob, while in Genesis Rabbah the great Judaic sages read the history of the children of Israel to the present.

We recall in this connection that while Scripture in the Book of Leviticus speaks of the sanctification of Israel, Leviticus Rabbah's framers transformed the Book of Leviticus into an account of Israel's salvation. This third type of Midrash-process or hermeneutic I call allegorical, meaning simply, reading one thing in light of some other, or parabolic or metaphorical for the same reason. The basic principle of Midrash-as-allegory is that things are never what they seem. Israel's reality is not conveyed either by the simple sense of Scripture or by the obvious realities of the perceived world. A deeper meaning in Scripture preserves the more profound meaning of the everyday world of Israel even now. This third type characterizes the rabbinic exegetes. The compilations Esther Rabbah, Lamentations Rabbah, Song of Songs Rabbah, and Ruth Rabbah contain numerous examples of the rereading of Scripture in light of the profound considerations of the moment, and the restructuring of the everyday within the paradigm of Scripture.

How, precisely, does Midrash-exegesis do its work? The verses of the written Torah that are quoted in rabbinic Midrash ordinarily shift from the meanings they convey to the implications they contain, thus speaking about something other than what they seem to be saying. The "as if" frame of mind brought to Scripture renews Scripture, with the sage seeing everything with fresh eyes. The result of the new vision was a reimagining of the social world envisioned by the document at hand, I mean, the everyday world of Israel in its land in that difficult time. What the sages proposed was a reconstruction of existence along the lines of the ancient design of Scripture as they read it. That meant that, from a sequence of one-time and linear events, everything that happened was turned into a repetition of known and already experienced paradigms, hence once more, a mythic being. The source and core of the myth, of course, derive from Scripture – Scripture reread, renewed, reconstructed along with the society that revered Scripture.

Reading one thing in terms of something else, the builders of the document systematically adopted for themselves the reality of the Scripture, its history and doctrines. They transformed that history from a sequence of one-time events, leading from one place to some other, into an ever-present mythic world. No longer was there one Moses, one David, one set of happenings of a distinctive and never-to-be-repeated character. Now whatever happened of which the thinkers propose to take account must enter and be absorbed into that established and ubiquitous pattern and structure founded in Scripture. It is not that biblical history repeats itself. Rather biblical history is no longer a story of things that happened long ago and pointed to some particular moment in the future. Biblical history becomes an account of things that happen every day – hence, an ever-present mythic world. That is why, in Midrash in the Judaism of the dual Torah, Scripture as a whole does not dictate the order of discourse, let alone its character. In this document the authors chose a verse here, a phrase there. In the more mature Midrash-compilations, such as Leviticus Rabbah and Pesiqta deRab Kahana, these then presented the pretext for propositional discourse commonly quite out of phase with the cited passage.

The framers of the Midrash-documents saw Scripture in a new way, just as they saw their own circumstance afresh. Specifically, they rejected their world in favor of Scripture's, reliving Scripture's world in their own terms. That, incidentally, is why they did not write history, an account of what was happening and what it meant. It was not that they did not recognize or appreciate important changes and trends reshaping their nation's life. They could not deny the realities. In their apocalyptic reading of the dietary and leprosy laws, as in Leviticus Rabbah, they made explicit their close encounter with the history of the world as they knew it. But they had another mode of responding to history – to treat history as if it were already known and readily understood. Whatever happened had already happened. Scripture dictated the contents of history, laying forth the structures of time, the rules that prevailed and were made known in events. Self-evidently, these same thinkers projected into Scripture's day the realities of their own, turning Moses and David into rabbis, for example. But that is how people think in that mythic, enchanted world in which, to begin with, reality blends with dream and hope projects onto future and past alike how people want things to be.

From these somewhat abstract observations we finally come to a concrete account of what happened, in particular, when the thinkers at hand undertook to reimagine reality, both their own and Scripture's. Exactly how did they think about one thing in terms of another, and what did they choose, in particular, to recognize in this rather complex process of juggling unpalatable present and unattainable myth? We take up the specifics by reverting to the tried and true method of listing all the data and classifying them. Exactly what did the framers of Midrash in the Judaism of the dual Torah learn when they opened Scripture? When they read the Scripture's rules of sanctification, they heard the message of the salvation of all Israel. Scripture became the story of how Israel, purified from social sin and sanctified, would be saved.

When, therefore, sages turned to historical events, reading them as other than what they seemed, and as they looked out upon the world of their day, they quite naturally appealed to Scripture's account of ancient Israel as the model and paradigm for all of history. The one-time events of the generation of the flood, Sodom and Gomorrah, the patriarchs and the sojourn in Egypt, the exodus, the revelation of the Torah at Sinai, the golden calf, the Davidic monarchy and the building of the Temple, Sennacherib, Hezekiah, the destruction of northern Israel, Nebuchadnezzar and the destruction of the Temple in 586, the life of Israel in Babylonian captivity, Daniel and his associates, Mordecai and Haman – these events occur over and over again in Midrash-compilations. They serve as paradigms of sin and atonement, steadfastness and divine intervention, and equivalent lessons. We find, in fact, a fairly standard repertoire of scriptural heroes or villains on the one side, and conventional lists of Israel's enemies and their actions and downfall on the other. The boastful, for instance, include the generation of the flood, Sodom and Gomorrah, Pharaoh, Sisera, Sennacherib, Nebuchadnezzar, the wicked empire (Rome) – contrasted to Israel, "despised and humble in this world." The four kingdoms recur again and again, always ending, of course, with Rome, with the repeated message that after Rome will come Israel. But Israel has to make this happen through its faith and submission to God's will. Lists of enemies ring the changes on Cain: the Sodomites, Pharaoh, Sennacherib, Nebuchadnezzar, Haman.

Accordingly, the mode of thought brought to bear upon the theme of history remains that of natural philosophy, that is, list-making, with data exhibiting similar taxonomic traits drawn together into lists based on common monothetic traits or definitions. These lists, through the power of repetition, make a single enormous point. They prove a social law of history. The catalogues of exemplary heroes and historical events serve a further purpose, providing a model of how contemporary events are to be absorbed into the biblical paradigm. Since biblical events exemplify recurrent happenings – sin and redemption, forgiveness and atonement – they lose their one-time character. At the same time and in the same way, current events find a place within the ancient but eternally present paradigmatic scheme.

History, then, is the future and not the past. No new historical events, other than exemplary episodes in lives of heroes, demand narration because, through what is said about the past, what was happening in the times of the framers of Midrash in the Judaism of the dual Torah would also come under consideration. This mode of dealing with biblical history and contemporary events produces two reciprocal effects. The first is the mythicization of biblical stories, their removal from the framework of ongoing, unique patterns of history and sequences of events and their transformation into accounts of things that happen all the time. The second is that contemporary events, too, lose all of their specificity and enter the paradigmatic framework of established mythic existence. So the Scripture's myth happens every day, and every day produces reenactment of the Scripture's myth.

Midrash shows us how the sages of the dual Torah mediated between God's word and their own world, equally and reciprocally invoking the one as a metaphor for the other. They learned from Scripture about what it meant for humanity to be "in our image, after our likeness," and they learned in the difficult world in which they lived how life in God's image of humanity, as set forth in

Scripture, was to be not only endured but lived in full holiness. It was to be the godly life on earth, life as the imitation of God. That theological conviction of the dual Torah frames a theology of culture, one that constantly refers to Scripture in the interpretation of everyday life, and to everyday life in the interpretation of Scripture. Such a theology of culture invokes both the eternal and continuing truths of Scripture and also the ephemeral but urgent considerations of the here and the now. Midrash, then, forms that bridge, defines that metaphor, and holds in the balance those two words of the here and now and the always. It reads the one in the light of the other, imparting one meaning to both, drawing each toward the plane of the other. Midrash reads the everyday as the metaphor against which the eternal is to be read, and the eternal as the metaphor against which the everyday is to be reenacted. In this fact I find a theological method pertinent to tomorrow's theologies of both Judaism and Christianity. Let me state matters with heavy emphasis.

There is a constant interplay, an ongoing interchange, between everyday affairs and the word of God in the Torah – Scripture. What we see reminds us of what Scripture says, and what Scripture says informs our understanding of the things we see and do in everyday life. That is what, in my view, the critical verse of Scripture, "In all thy ways, know Him," means. The deep structure of human existence, framed by Scripture and formed out of God's will as spelled out in the Torah, forms the foundation of our everyday life. Here and now, in the life of the hour, we can and do know God. So everyday life forms a commentary on revealed Scripture – on the Torah – and Scripture, the Torah, provides a commentary on everyday life. Life flows in both directions.

The sages exercised freedom of interpretation by insisting that God speaks through the Torah to Israel everywhere and continually. When they brought to the written Torah the deepest anguish of the age, they allowed that component of the Torah to speak to them in the here and now. The bridge they built brought traffic in both directions, from today to Sinai, from Sinai to the present moment. That is what I mean when I represent Midrash as mediator. The principal mode of thinking in Midrash translates the metaphor into a policy of culture. It requires us to look deeply at something since, in the depths, we find something else, as each thing stands for another, and all things possess a potentiality of meaning never close to the surface but always in the depths of God's revealed will in the Torah. That account of the continuity of culture under the aspect of Midrash leads us to the limits of this world, which mark the bottom boundary at the threshold of the other. With the formation of the Midrash-compilations, the written Torah and the oral Torah were beginning to unite. In the pages of the Talmud of Babylonia or Bavli, the two Torahs are made one, and the Judaism of the dual Torah reaches its classic and authoritative statement.

7

The Dual Torah in its Unitary Statement:
The Bavli

When people speak of "the Talmud," they mean not the Talmud of the Land of Israel ("the Yerushalmi") of about 400 CE, but the Talmud of Babylonia ("the Bavli") brought to closure about 600 CE. The latter document, comprising discourses on thirty-seven of the Mishnah's sixty-two tractates (not all of them the same tractates as are dealt with by the Yerushalmi), constitutes the *summa* and the complete statement of the Judaism of the dual Torah as it was defined in its formative age. From the early seventh century when the Bavli was closed, to the present day, the Judaism of the dual Torah has continued its long history always within the boundaries – mythic, symbolic, normative in theology and conduct alike – of that protean writing. Commentaries and commentaries upon commentaries, codes of law, authoritative *ad hoc* decisions (*"responsa"*) – these three kinds of writing expanded and developed the Bavli's basic principles.

Philosophers and theologians appealed not only to its authority, but to its doctrine. Lawyers and judges governed Israel, the Jewish people, by reference to the document read as a constitution. In some times and places, ordinary people expressed their love for God and the Torah by studying the lines of this writing. If there is one document that is Judaism, it *is* the Bavli. All of contemporary Orthodox Judaisms concur; Conservative and Reconstructionist Judaisms do not vastly differ except in detail; and Reform Judaism agrees in principle that the Bavli is a primary source of theological truth requiring exposition, if not invariably demanding assent.

Yet, to tell the history of this particular Judaism, we find it difficult to point within the Bavli to developments of such originality and innovative character as to explain its influence. The foundation document should, after all, comprise the Yerushalmi, together perhaps with Genesis Rabbah and Leviticus Rabbah. Among those three compilations we can locate every important idea that the Bavli later set forth. Surely some of the principal Midrash-compilations should find a place alongside the Bavli as principal writings. Yet while all of these documents fall into the category of oral Torah, none has ever attained the stature, in the mind of the faith and the lives of the faithful, of the Bavli.

If we want to know why that is the case, we must ask what distinguishes the Bavli from any prior writing. The answer is simple. The Bavli's framers brought together within a single piece of writing both the Mishnah and its required amplification, and Scripture and its required amplification. They joined the written Torah, as they wished it to be read, and the oral Torah, as they proposed to lay it out. Within the pages that the Bavli's framers composed, they set forth in proportion and in place the one whole Torah of Moses, our rabbi, that (within their mythic framework) God had revealed at Sinai. The Bavli, therefore, represents a triumph of composition and conclusion, a classic comprising the classics. While much that its framers said was fresh and important on its own, and while they accomplished far more than a mere paraphrase and summary of received materials, their principal contribution lay not in innovation but in the authoritative re-presentation of what could now plausibly be called "the tradition."

By joining the whole and providing a reprise of all of the parts, the authorship of the Bavli imparted to the Judaism of the dual Torah the quality of tradition, something handed on from prophet to sage, as Mishnah-tractate Avot represents matters. In the form of tradition, that fresh and remarkable system framed in the Yerushalmi and its associated writings would pass forward through the ages: new ideas once, established truth of Sinai now. The Bavli's definitive reshaping of the Judaism of the dual Torah constituted more than a work of literary legerdemain. In its pages we have far more than a mere reprise of what we find in the Yerushalmi and important Midrash-compilations. If, however, we wish to understand the chapter in the history of Judaism written in the Bavli, we must focus upon the accomplishment in formulation and redaction of received materials from the Mishnah, the Tosefta, the Yerushalmi, and the principal Midrash-compilations of the framers of the Bavli. That is where they made their mark, and that is, more importantly, why their document took priority over all others before *and afterward*.

What precisely did the authorship of the Bavli accomplish? If we want to know what and how people thought, we begin by asking how they organized what they knew and about the choices they made in laying out the main lines of the structure of knowledge. When we approach a document so vast and complex as the Bavli, resting as it does on a still larger and more complex antecedent corpus of writings, we do best to begin at the very beginning.

Before the time of the Bavli's authors, three principles of composition and redaction – Mishnah exegesis, Scripture exegesis, and biographical collection – flourished more or less in isolation from one another. How do we know? The first is fully exposed in the Talmud of the Land of Israel; the second in earlier compilations of scriptural exegeses. The third accounts for the available biographical composites. It is clear, therefore, that the antecedent authors of sizable passages (ten or twenty connected paragraphs) and redactors, before the age of the Bavli's own compositors, thought that the three things could be done fairly separately.

Accordingly, we must review the choices made by prior authorships in collecting, organizing, and laying out completed writings – for example, stories, comments on verses of Scripture, sayings, amplifications of paragraphs of the Mishnah and of the Tosefta in relationship to the Mishnah, and the like. What had others done and what did this authorship do? When the final organizers of the Talmud of Babylonia considered the redactional choices made by their predecessors, two appeared the most likely. First, the organizers might take up and arrange such materials as they had in their hands around the categories of Scripture – books or verses or themes – as had their precursors in bringing into being compositions made up of exegeses of Scripture (Midrashim). Or they might follow the order of the Mishnah and compose a systematic commentary and amplification of Scripture, as had their precursors who created the Talmud of the Land of Israel a century or so before.

When they considered their task, however, they recognized that they had in hand a tripartite corpus of inherited materials awaiting composition into a final, closed document. First, they took up materials in various states and stages of completion that were pertinent to the Mishnah or to the principles or laws that the Mishnah had originally brought to articulation. Second, they received materials, again in various conditions, pertinent to the Scripture, both as the Scripture related to the Mishnah and also as the Scripture laid forth its own narratives. Finally, they had materials focused on sages. These were framed around twin biographical principles, either as strings of stories about great sages of the past or as collections of sayings and comments drawn together solely because the same name stood behind the sayings. No one had earlier compiled stories about holy men into biographies as had Christian authors ("gospels" or "lives of saints"). For many centuries to come, until the advent of the Hasidic revision of the dual Torah in the early nineteenth century, no one wrote lives of saints.[1]

The framers of the Bavli decided to adopt and join in a single document the two redactional principles inherited from the antecedent century and to reject the one already rejected by their predecessors, even while honoring it. First, they organized the Bavli around the Mishnah. Thirty-seven tractates were given amplifications that were in part commentaries, expansions and generalizations, or sustained speculative essays covering varieties of legal topics. Approximately sixty per cent of the bulk of the Bavli tractates, in a probe I made of five of the thirty-seven, serve as expansions of the Mishnah.[2]

Second, they adapted and included vast amounts of antecedent materials organized as scriptural commentary. They inserted these whole and complete, not at all in response to the Mishnah's program. Approximately forty per cent of the bulk of the Bavli comprises this kind of material.[3] In these passages the logic of redaction – what self-evidently comes first, what obviously goes below – emerges from a different sort of exegetical task than a Mishnah commentary. Here people focused upon passages of Scripture as they drafted their exegetical compositions. Verse-by-verse amplifications, in the model

---

[1] The earliest lives of the Baal Shem Tov, the founder of Hasidism, and his principal heirs were published in the early nineteenth century. The stories, of course, circulated earlier, just as stories about great sages and other holy men circulated in prior centuries but were not made into biographies or compiled and organized in other ways.

[2] See my *Judaism. The Classical Statement. The Evidence of the Bavli* (Chicago: University of Chicago Press, 1986).

[3] Here the proportions vary considerably from tractate to tractate.

of the treatment of the Mishnah's sentences and paragraphs, were strung together.

Finally, while making provision for compositions built upon biographical principles, preserving strings of sayings from a given master (and often a tradent of a given master) and tales about authorities of the preceding half millennium, they accomplished nothing new. That is, they never created redactional compositions of a sizable order that focused upon given authorities, even though sufficient materials were at hand to do so.

In the three decisions – two concerning what to do and one about what not to do – the final compositors of the Bavli indicated what they proposed to accomplish: to give final form and fixed expression, through their categories of the organization of all knowledge, to the Torah as it had been known, sifted, searched, approved, and handed down, even from the remote past to their own day. In our literary categories, then, the compositors of the Bavli were encyclopaedists. Their creation became the encyclopaedia of Judaism, its *summa*, its point of final reference, its court of last appeal, its definition, its conclusion, its closure – so they thought and so said those that followed to this very day.

Accordingly, the framers of the Bavli drew together the results of three types of work that people prior to their own labors had already created in abundance. Using the two I specified as definitive redactional structures, the framers made them one document, the Bavli, or in the later tradition of Judaism, the Talmud. Whatever the place and role of the diverse types of compositions circulating before and in the time of the Bavli – compilations of scriptural exegeses, the Yerushalmi, not to mention the exegeses of Pentateuchal laws in Sifra and the Sifres, the Tosefta, Pirqe Abot and Abot de R. Natan, and on and on – the Bavli superseded all. It took pride of place. It laid the final seal upon the past and defined not only what would succeed for an unknown tomorrow but the very form, topical order, and program of all that would pass into the hands of the future.

Since the first of the two Talmuds (the Yerushalmi) provided the model for the way in which the Bavli's authorship would treat the Mishnah, let us review its legacy. In many ways it defined how the Mishnah would be read in the Bavli. The Yerushalmi invariably does to the Mishnah one of the following: 1. textual criticism; 2. exegesis of the meaning of the Mishnah, including glosses and amplifications; 3. addition of scriptural prooftexts regarding the Mishnah's central propositions; and 4. harmonization of one Mishnah passage with another such passage, or with a statement of Tosefta. These four taxa encompass all of the Yerushalmi's units of discourse that relate to the Mishnah, ninety per cent of the whole of the Yerushalmi. The first two of these four procedures remain wholly within the narrow frame of the Mishnah passage subject to discussion. The second pair take an essentially independent stance *vis-à-vis* the Mishnah pericope at hand.

The Mishnah is read by the Yerushalmi as a composite of discrete and essentially autonomous rules – a set of atoms and not an integrated molecule, so to speak. In this way the most striking formal traits of the Mishnah are obliterated. More important, the Mishnah as a whole and complete statement of a viewpoint no longer exists. Its propositions are reduced to details. On occasion, the details may be restated in generalizations encompassing a wide variety of other details across the gaps between one tractate and another. This immensely creative and imaginative approach to the Mishnah vastly expands the range of discourse. But the first and deepest consequence is to deny to the Mishnah its own mode of speech and its distinctive and coherent message. The authorship of the Bavli did no less. Where the Bavli's and the Yerushalmi's framers differ is in the treatment of history and biography. The Yerushalmi contains a number of statements that something happened or narratives about how something happened. Stories about and rules for sages and disciples, separate from discussion of a passage of the Mishnah, also occur in the Yerushalmi. Preserved but parsimoniously in the Yerushalmi, these same kinds of materials make massive contributions to the Bavli. The difference, however, is in proportion and not in substance.

How about the comparison of the Bavli's treatment of passages of Scripture with the disposition of Scripture in Midrash-compilations? The taxonomical categories for a Midrash-compilation's treatment of a scriptural book are four, of which the first two are closely related and the fourth of slight consequence. The first category encompasses close exegesis of Scripture, by which I mean a word-for-word or phrase-by-phrase interpretation of a passage. In such an activity, the framer of a discrete composition will wish to read and explain a verse or a few words of a verse of the Scripture at hand. The second category, no less exegetical than the first, is made up of units of discourse in which the components of the verse are treated as part of a larger statement of meaning rather than as a set of individual phrases, stichs requiring attention one by one. Accordingly, in this taxon we deal with wide-ranging discourse about the meaning of a particular passage, hence an effort to amplify what is said in a verse. The amplification may take a number of different forms and directions. But the discipline imposed by the originally cited verse of Scripture will always impose boundaries on discourse.

The useful third taxon encompasses units of discourse in which the theme of a particular passage defines a wide-ranging exercise. In this discussion the cited passage itself is unimportant; it is the theme that is definitive. Accordingly, we take up a unit of discourse in which the composer of the passage wishes to expand on a particular problem, which is merely illustrated in the cited passage. The problem, rather than the cited passage, defines the limits and direction of discourse. The passage at hand falls away, having provided a mere pretext for the real point of concern. The fourth and final taxon, also deriving from the Yerushalmi, takes in units of discourse shaped around a given topic but not intended to constitute cogent and tightly framed discourse on the topic. These units of discourse constitute topical anthologies rather than carefully composed essays.

The Bavli contains materials of these four types. In the nature of things, the Bavli's framers did not compose tractates around biblical books. But they did assemble enormous compositions on sustained passages of biblical books. The result is that in the pages of the Bavli, as much as in Midrash-compilations, we study Scripture in the way in which the sages wished Scripture to be read: as part of the Torah, the one whole Torah of Moses our rabbi.

The Yerushalmi and the collections of scriptural exegeses include compositions of already-worked-out units of discourse focused upon the Mishnah and Scripture respectively. Other such completed compositions deal with individual sages. The two cited components of the canon of Judaism as well as the Bavli contain a sizable quantity of sage units of discourse. These could have coalesced in yet a third type of book. Specifically, sayings and stories about sages could have been organized into collections of wise sayings attributed to various authorities (like Abot) on the one side, or brief snippets of biographies or lives of the saints on the other. No one made such compilations.

But the Bavli's framers found ample space for them, proportionately and actually far larger than the accommodations for biographical materials supplied in the Yerushalmi and in the Midrash-compilations.

Accommodating biographical materials served the purpose of forming a complete and classic statement. For precisely the same modes of explanation and interpretation found suitable for the Mishnah and the Scripture served equally well for the sayings and doings of sages. That fact may be shown in three ways. First, just as Scripture supplied prooftexts, so deeds or statements of sages served as prooftexts. Second, just as a verse of Scripture or an explicit statement of the Mishnah resolved a disputed point, so also what a sage said or did might be introduced into discourse as ample proof for settling a dispute. Third, it follows that just as Scripture or the Mishnah laid down Torah, so also what a sage did or said laid down Torah. In the dimensions of the applied and practical reason by which the law unfolded, the sage found a comfortable place in precisely the taxonomic categories defined by the Mishnah and Scripture.

An example of the kind of sustained discourse that appears in biographical materials produced by circles of sages follows. As these circles composed units of discourse about the meaning of a Mishnah passage, a larger theoretical problem of law, the sense of scriptural verse, or the sayings and doings of scriptural heroes seen as sages, so they composed the same for living sages themselves. In the simplest example, we see that two discrete sayings of a sage are joined together. The principle of conglomeration, therefore, is solely the name of the sage at hand. One saying deals with overcoming the impulse to do evil and the other with the classifications of sages' programs of learning. What the two subjects have in common is slight, but that fact meant nothing to the framer of the passage. He thought that compositions joined by the same tradent and authority – Levi and Simeon – should be made up.

A. Said R.Levi bar Hama and R. Simeon b. Laqish, "A person should always provoke his impulse to do good against his impulse to do evil,

B. "as it is said, 'Provoke and do not sin' (Ps. 4:5).

C. "If [the good impulse] wins, well and good. If not, let him take up Torah study?

D. "as it is said, 'Commune with your own heart' (Ps. 4:5).

E. "If [the good impulse'] wins, well and good. If not, let him recite the Shema,

F. "as it is said, 'upon your bed' (Ps. 4:5).

G. "If [the good impulse] wins, well and good. If not, let him remember the day of death,

H. "as it is said, 'And keep silent. Sela' (Ps. 4:5)."

I. And R. Levi bar Hama said R. Simeon b. Laqish said, "What is the meaning of the verse of Scripture, 'And I will give you the tables of stone, the law and the commandment, which I have written, that you may teach them' (Exod. 24:12)?

J. "'The tables' refers to the Ten Commandments.

K. "'Torah' refers to Scripture.

L. "'Commandment' refers to Mishnah.

M. "'Which I have written' refers to the Prophets and the Writings.

N. "'That you may teach them' refers to the Gemara.

O. "This teaches that all of them were given to Moses from Sinai."

Babylonian Talmud Tractate Berakhot 4B.XXIII.

The frame of the story at hand links A to H and I to O in a way unfamiliar to those accustomed to the principles of conglomeration in legal and biblical-exegetical compositions. In the former, a given problem or principle of law will tell us why one item is joined to some other. In the latter, a single verse of Scripture will account for the joining of two or more otherwise discrete units of thought. Here one passage, A to H, takes up Ps. 4:5; the other, I to O, takes up Exod. 24:12. The point of the one statement hardly goes over the ground of the other. So the sole principle by which one item has joined the other is biographical – a record of what a sage said about topics that are, at best, contiguous, if related at all. This example of how stories about sages were collected and organized in the Bavli suffices to show the importance assigned to tales of holy men[4] in the Bavli. When, therefore, we understand how this document brought together

---

[4] Few holy women occur.

a variety of different types of documents and materials and made them into one, we see in a detailed way the character of the framers' work.

Why did the framers of the Bavli not trouble with biographical tractates? We, of course, cannot answer that question by consulting diaries or notes or transcripts of discussions. Logic, however, suggests an answer. Either a teaching was true and authoritative wherever it was found and however it had reached the living sage, or a teaching was untrue and not authoritative. Scripture, the Mishnah, the sage – the three spoke with equal authority. True, one had to come into alignment with the other – the Mishnah with Scripture and the sage with the Mishnah. But it was not the case that one component of the Torah stood within the sacred circle and another beyond. Interpretation and what was interpreted, exegesis and text, belonged together. Once the Torah was deemed both written and oral, then one component of the Torah would remain wholly in unwritten form, not preserved in writing at all. By definition it could not be Scripture. But it also could not be the Mishnah or the Midrash-compilations. For, quite clearly, hundreds of years of writing down passages of the oral Torah had already passed. So the one component of the tripartite Torah – oral, written, living – that would remain in oral form would have to be the sage – living through time through the preservation in oral and not redacted form of the things he did and said. The sage then lived on in the life of the faithful – the never-to-be-written-down component of the Torah, enduring as long as the Torah would last, that is, time immemorial.

That decision placed the sage at the center of the Torah, for the sage speaks with authority about the Mishnah and the Scripture. He therefore has authority deriving from revelation and may himself participate in the process of revelation. There is no material difference. Since that is the case, the sage's book, whether the Yerushalmi or the Bavli to the Mishnah or Midrash to Scripture, is Torah, that is, revealed by God. It also forms part of the Torah and is a fully canonical document. The sage is thus like Moses, "our rabbi," who received torah and wrote the Torah. While the canon was in three parts – Scripture, Mishnah, sage – the sage, in saying what the other parts meant and in embodying that meaning in his life and thought, took primacy of place. If no document organized itself around sayings and stories of sages, it was because that was superfluous. Why?

Because all documents equally, whether Scripture, Mishnah, or Yerushalmi, gave full and complete expression regarding the deeds and deliberations of sages beginning with Moses.

Would that judgment have surprised the authorship of the Yerushalmi? Not at all. They too preserved stories of sages, if not in so prominent a position as did the Bavli's framers. There is only one important difference between the two Talmuds, but that difference suffices to explain the power of the Bavli to define the Torah. The distinction lies solely in the redactional character of the Bavli. The difference between the Bavli and the Yerushalmi is the Bavli's far more ample use of Scripture not only for proof, but for the redaction and organization of large-scale discourse. In the Bavli the Scripture serves alongside the Mishnah and is not enormously less than it in volume. Scripture and the Mishnah together in the Bavli define structure and impart proportion and organization. In the Yerushalmi, by contrast, Scripture forms an important component of the canon, but it does not dictate lines of order and main beams of structure. What difference does this distinction between the two Talmuds actually make?

The Bavli's complete union in its redactional substrate of the Mishnah and Scripture, encompassing also exemplary actions and sayings of sages, provided a summa of Judaism. The authorship of the Bavli thereby joined the two streams that, like the Missouri and the Mississippi Rivers at St Louis, had until its time flowed separately and distinct from one another within the same banks. The one stream, coursing from the source of the Mishnah, and the other stream, emanating from the source of Scripture, had mingled only in eddies, at the edges. But the banks of the mighty river had been set from Sinai and, in the mythic dimension, the two streams had been meant to flow together as one river. In the Yerushalmi, Scripture found a place along the sides; the Mishnah formed the main stream. In the collections of scriptural exegesis (midrashim), Scripture had flowed by itself down the center, wholly apart from the Mishnah. In the Bavli, for the first time, the waters not only flowed together but mingled in the middle and in the depths, in common and sustained discourse. So the Bavli for the first time from Sinai (to speak within the Torah myth) joined together in a whole and complete way, in literary form and in doctrinal substance, the one whole Torah of Moses.

That is why the Bavli became the Torah *par excellence*, the Torah through which Israel would read both Scripture and Mishnah, the Torah all together, the Torah all at once, as God at Sinai had revealed it to Moses, our rabbi. It was because the Bavli's writers accomplished the near perfect union of Scripture and Mishnah in a single document that the Bavli became Israel's fullest Torah. That is why when the people of the Torah, Israel, the Jewish people, for the next fifteen hundred years, wished to approach the Mishnah, it was through the reading of the Bavli. That is why when that same people wished to address Scripture, it was through the reading of the Bavli. All the other components of the canon, while authentic and authoritative too, stood in line from second place backward, behind the primary reading of the Bavli. It is no accident that authentic avatars of the classical literature of Judaism even today learn Scripture through the Bavli's citations of verses of Scripture just as much as, commonly, they learn the Mishnah and assuredly interpret it exactly as the Bavli presents it.

It was for good reason that the Bavli has formed the definitive statement of Judaism from the time of its closure to the present day. The excellence of its composition, the mastery and authority of those who everywhere studied it and advocated its law, the sharpness of its exegesis and discussion, the harmonious and proportionate presentation of all details, these virtues of taste and intellect may well have secured for the document its paramount position. The Babylonian Talmud, moreover, incorporated a far broader selection of antecedent materials than any other document that reaches us out of Judaism in late antiquity, far more, for instance, than the Yerushalmi. This vast selection was so organized and assembled that systematic accounts of numerous important problems of biblical exegesis, law and theology alike, emerged. Consequently, the Bavli served from its closure as an encyclopedia of knowledge and as a *summa* of the theology and law of Judaism. The comprehensive character of the Bavli, in form and in substance, and its dependence upon the Scripture's and the Mishnah's redactional framework, gained for it the priority it would enjoy. No one had done what the Bavli did before; no one had to do it again. The Torah was now complete.

— 8 —

The Symbol of Torah

With the completion of the Bavli, the dual Torah had reached its full literary statement. But what about the symbol of Torah that differentiates the Judaism of the dual Torah from all others and unites all of the phenomena of this Judaism into a single coherent statement? We turn now from the writings that portray the system to the symbol that, wholly on its own, fully expresses and evokes that same system.

The symbol in literary form reaches us in an odd formulation: "torah," not "*the* Torah." The symbol, Torah, in the Judaism of the dual Torah, reached its verbal formulation when "the Torah" lost its capital letter and definite article and ultimately became "torah." An important usage of the word torah in the Bavli captures the shift from a particular object, a book or scroll, to a totally other sense:

> A. R. Kahana [a disciple] went and hid under the bed of Rab [his master.]
> B. Hearing Rab "discoursing" and joking with his wife, [Kahana] said to [Rab], "You would think that Abba's [Rab's] mouth had never before tasted 'the dish.'"
> C. [Rab] said to [Kahana], "Kahan, are you down there? Get out! This is a disgrace!"
> D. [Kahana] said to [Rab], "My lord, it is a matter of Torah, and I have the need to learn."
>
> Babylonian Talmud tractate Berakhot P. 62A

The study of Torah need not encompass cultic voyeurism, but here "torah" encompasses the manner in which a holy man has sexual relations (complete with cunnilingus).

The shift in the sense of Torah now is self-evident, though to analyze what has changed and why demands some attention. The word "torah" denotes not only the Torah, the five Books of Moses, or "the oral and written Torah," but also a status and a category. Many things could and did enjoy the status of torah or fall into the classification of torah. Words, things, deeds, persons – all could be torah. What for nearly a millennium had been a particular scroll or book thus came to serve as a symbol of an entire system. When a rabbi spoke of torah, he no longer meant only a particular object, for example, a scroll and its contents. Now he used the word to encompass a distinctive and well-defined world-view and way of life. Torah had come to stand for something one does. Knowledge of the Torah promised not merely information about what people were supposed to do, but connoted the status of a person or a gesture or thing; and torah-status further connoted ultimate redemption or salvation.

When we speak of torah in the rabbinical literature of late antiquity, we no longer denote a particular book or the contents of such a book. Instead, we connote a broad range of clearly distinct categories of noun and verb, concrete fact and abstract relationship. Torah stands for a kind of human being. It connotes a social status and a social group. It refers to a type of social relationship. It further denotes a legal status and differentiates among legal norms. As symbolic abstraction, the word encompasses things and persons, actions and status, points of social differentiation and legal and normative standing, as well as revealed truth.

In all, the main points of insistence of the whole of Israel's life and history come to full symbolic expression in that single word. If people wanted to explain how they would be saved, they would use the word torah. If they wished to sort out their parlous relationships with gentiles, they would use the word torah. Torah stood for salvation and accounted for Israel's this-worldly condition and the hope, for individual and nation alike, of life in the world to come. For the kind of Judaism under discussion, the word torah stood for everything. The Torah symbolized the whole, at once and entire. When, therefore, we wish to describe the unfolding of the definitive doctrine of Judaism in its formative period, the first exercise consists in paying close attention to the meanings imputed to a single word.

Every detail of the religious system at hand exhibits essentially the same point of insistence, captured in the simple notion of the

Torah as the generative symbol, the total, exhaustive expression of the system as a whole. That is why the definitive ritual of the Judaism under consideration consisted in studying the Torah. That is why the definitive myth explained that one who studied Torah would become holy, like Moses "our rabbi," and like God, in whose image humanity was made and whose Torah provided the plan and the model for what God wanted of a humanity created in his image. As Christians found the image of God in Christ, God made flesh, so the framers of the this Judaism found in the Torah that image of God to which Israel should aspire, and to which the sage in fact conformed.

The meaning of the several meanings of the Torah should require only brief explanation.

When the Torah refers to a particular thing, it is to a scroll containing divinely revealed words.

The Torah may further refer to revelation, not as an object but as a corpus of doctrine.

When one "does Torah," the disciple "studies" or "learns," and the master "teaches" Torah. Hence while the word torah never appears as a verb, it does refer to an act.

The word also bears a quite separate sense, that is, torah as category or classifiction or corpus of rules. "The torah of driving a car", for example, is a usage entirely acceptable to some documents.

The word torah very commonly refers to a status, distinct from and above another status, for example, "teachings of the Torah" as against "teachings of the scribes." For the two Talmuds, that distinction is absolutely critical to the entire hermeneutic enterprise; it is important even in the Mishnah.

Obviously, no account of the meaning of the word torah can ignore the distinction between the two Torahs, written and oral. It is important only in the secondary stages of the formation of the literature.

Finally, the word torah refers to a source of salvation, often fully worked out in stories about how the individual and the nation will be saved through Torah. In general, the sense of the word "salvation" is not complicated. It is simply salvation in the way in which Deuteronomy and the Deuteronomic historians understand it: kings who do what God wants win battles; those who do not, lose. So also here, people who study and do Torah are saved from sickness and

death, and the way Israel can save itself from its condition of
degradation also is through Torah.

Can we account for the history of the development of the symbol
– expressed in word, deed (or refraining from a deed), attitude, and
conviction? As with all matters, we begin with the initial document
of the Judaism of the dual Torah to answer our question. The
Mishnah provides no account of itself. Unlike biblical law codes, the
Mishnah begins with no myth of its own origin. It ends with no
doxology. Discourse commences in the middle of things and ends
abruptly. What follows from such laconic mumbling is that the exact
status of the document required definition entirely outside the
framework of the document itself. The framers of the Mishnah gave
no hint of the nature of their book, so the Mishnah reached the
political world of Israel without a trace of self-conscious explanation
or any theory of validation. The one thing that is clear, alas, is
negative.

The framers of the Mishnah nowhere claim, implicitly or explicitly,
that what they wrote forms part of the Torah, enjoys the status of
God's revelation to Moses at Sinai, or even systematically carries
forward secondary exposition and application of what Moses wrote
down in the wilderness. Later on, two hundred years beyond the
close of the Mishnah, the need to explain the standing and origin of
the Mishnah led some to posit two things: 1. God's revelation of the
Torah at Sinai encompassed the Mishnah as much as Scripture; and
2. the Mishnah was handed on through oral formulation and oral
transmission from Sinai to the framers of the document as we have
it. One part was in writing. The other was oral and now is in
the Mishnah. Once the Mishnah could fall into the category or
classification of Scripture, then the Torah (meaning the Hebrew
Scriptures or the Pentateuch) no longer enjoyed definitive standing.
The Torah as a particular book gave way to torah as a status that
diverse writings might enjoy, and at that moment the boundaries
around the Torah gave way. Torah began as a metaphor: the
Mishnah falls into the category of the Pentateuchal Torah because
it presents sayings that were received in a chain of tradition from
Sinai. So the Mishnah is connected with the Torah and it is like the
Torah. In that sense, the Mishnah is torah. That metaphorization
of the Torah into torah forms the first step; from that point, all else
was inevitable. From metaphor, torah shaded over into symbol.

As for the Mishnah itself, however, it contains not a hint that anyone has heard a tale that would convey the meaning of torah as metaphor, let alone myth and (simultaneously, of course) symbol. The earliest apologists for the Mishnah, represented in Abot and the Tosefta, know nothing of the fully realized myth of the dual Torah of Sinai. It may be that the authors of those documents stood too close to the Mishnah to see the Mishnah's standing as a problem or to recognize the task of accounting for its origins. Certainly they never refer to the Mishnah as something out there, nor speak of the document as autonomous and complete. Only the two Talmuds reveal that conception – alongside their mythic explanation of where the document came from and why it should be obeyed. So the Yerushalmi marks the change. In any event, the absence of explicit expression of such a claim in behalf of the Mishnah requires little specification. It is just not there.

But the absence of an implicit claim demands explanation. When ancient Jews wanted to gain for their writings the status of revelation, of torah, or at least to link what they thought to what the Torah had said, they could do one of four things: 1. they could sign the name of a holy man of old, for instance, Adam, Enoch, Ezra; 2. they could imitate the Hebrew style of Scripture; 3. they could claim that God had spoken to them; or 4. they could, at the very least, cite a verse of Scripture and impute to the cited passage their own opinion. These four methods – pseudepigraphy, stylistic imitation (hence, forgery), claim of direct revelation from God, and eisegesis – found no favour with the Mishnah's framers. To the contrary, they signed no name to their book. Their Hebrew was new in its syntax and morphology, completely unlike that of the Mosaic writings of the Pentateuch. They never claimed that God had anything to do with their opinions. They rarely cited a verse of Scripture as authority. Whatever the authors of the Mishnah said about their document, the implicit character of the books tells us that they did not claim God had dictated or even approved what they had to say. The framers simply ignored all the validating conventions of the world in which they lived.

A survey of the uses of the word torah in the Mishnah, to be sure, provides us with an account of what the framers of the Mishnah (founders of what would emerge as rabbinic Judaism) understood by that term. Such a survey, however, will not tell us how they related their own ideas to the Torah, nor shall we find a trace of evidence of that fully articulated way of life – the use of the word Torah to categorize and classify persons, places, things, relationships, all manner of abstractions – that we find fully exposed in some later redacted writings. True, the Mishnah places a high value upon studying the Torah and upon the status of the sage. A *"mamzer-disciple* of a sage takes priority over a high-priest *amthaares"* (M. Hor. 3:8). But that judgment, distinctive though it is, cannot settle the question. All it shows is that the Mishnah pays due honor to the sage. If the Mishnah does not claim to constitute part of the Torah, then what makes a sage a sage is not mastery of the Mishnah in particular.

Abot draws into the orbit of Torah-talk the names of authorities of the Mishnah. While, to be sure, Abot does not claim that the Mishnah forms part of the Torah, in Abot, Torah is instrumental. The figure of the sage, his ideals and conduct, forms the goal, focus, and center. Abot regards study of Torah as what a sage does. The substance of Torah is what a sage says. That is so whether or not the saying relates to scriptural revelation. The content of the sayings attributed to sages endows those sayings with self-validating status. The sages usually do not quote verses of Scripture and explain them, nor do they speak in God's name. Yet it is clear sages talk Torah. Therefore, if a sage says something, what he says is Torah. More accurately, what he says falls into the classification of Torah.

Accordingly Abot treats Torah-learning as symptomatic, as an indicator of the status of the sage, and as merely instrumental. The simplest proof of that proposition lies in the recurrent formal structure of the document, which we have already consulted. It is marked by the one thing the framers of the document never omit and always emphasize: 1. the name of the authority behind a saying, from Simeon the Righteous on downward, and 2. the connective-attributive "says." So what is important to the redactors is what they never have to tell us. Because a recognized sage makes a statement, what he says constitutes in and of itself a statement in the status of Torah. The theory of Abot pertains to the religious standing and consequence of the learning of the sages. To be sure, a secondary effect of that theory endows things sages say with the status of revealed truth. This is because they say them, not because they have heard them in an endless chain back to Sinai. The fundament of truth passes on through sagacity, not through already-formulated and carefully-memorized truths. That is why the single most important word in Abot also is the most common, the word "says."

At issue in Abot is not the Torah but the authority of the sage. That authority transforms a saying into a Torah-saying or, to state matters more appropriately, it places a saying into the classification of the Torah. Abot then stands as the first document of the doctrine that the sage embodies the Torah and is a holy man, like Moses "our rabbi," in the likeness and image of God. The process begins with the claim that a saying falls into the category of Torah if a sage says it as Torah. It ends with the view that the sage himself is Torah incarnate. We have already met these sages in the pages of the Bavli, who form the main beam of the Judaism of the dual Torah in its foundations and structure.

The Mishnah is regarded in the Talmud of the Land of Israel as equivalent to Scripture. But the Mishnah is not called Torah. Still, once the Mishnah entered the status of Scripture, it was only a short step to regard it as part of the revelation at Sinai – hence, oral Torah.

In the first Talmud we find the glimmerings of an effort to theorize in general, not merely in detail, about how specific teachings of Mishnah relate to specific teachings of Scripture. The citing of scriptural proof texts for Mishnah propositions, after all, would not have caused much surprise to the framers of the Mishnah; they themselves included such passages, though not often. But what conception of the Torah underlies such initiatives, and how do Yerushalmi sages propose to explain the phenomenon of the Mishnah as a whole? The following passage gives us one statement. It refers to the assertion at M. Hag. 1:8D that the laws on cultic cleanness presented in the Mishnah rest on deep and solid foundations in the Scripture.

[VA] The laws of the Sabbath [M. 1:8B]: R. Jonah said R. Hama bar Uqba raised the question [in reference to M. Hag. 1:8D's view that there are many verses of Scripture on cleanness], "And lo, it is written only, 'Nevertheless a spring or a cistern holding water shall be clean; but whatever touches their carcass shall be unclean' (Lev. 11:36). And from this verse you derive many laws. [So how can M. 8:8D say what it does about many verses for laws of cultic cleanness?]"

[B] R. Zeira in the name of R. Yohanan; "If a law comes to hand and you do not know its nature, do not discard it for another one, for lo, many laws were stated to Moses at Sinai, and all of them have been embedded in the Mishnah."

Y. Hagigah 1:7

The truly striking assertion appears at B. The Mishnah is now said to contain statements made by God to Moses. Just how these statements found their way into the Mishnah, and which passages of the Mishnah contain them, we do not know. That is hardly important, given the fundamental assertion at hand. The passage proceeds to a further and far more consequential proposition. It asserts that part of the Torah was written down, and part was preserved in memory and transmitted orally. In context, moreover, that distinction must encompass the Mishnah, thus explaining its origin as part of the Torah. Here is a clear and unmistakable expression of the distinction between two forms in which a single Torah was revealed and handed on at Mount Sinai, part in writing and part orally.

While the passage below does not make use of the language, that is, Torah-in-writing and Torah-by-memory, it does refer to "the written" and "the oral." It seems fully justifiable to supply the word Torah in square brackets. The reader will note, however, that the word Torah likewise does not occur at K, L. Only when the passage reaches its climax at M does it break down into a number of categories – Scripture, Mishnah, Talmud, laws, lore. There it makes the additional point that everything comes from Moses at Sinai. So the fully articulated theroy of two Torahs (not merely one Torah in two forms) does not reach final expression in this passage. But short of explicit allusion to Torah-in-writing and Torah-by-memory, which as far as I am able to discern, we find mainly in the Talmud of Babylonia, the ultimate theory of Torah of formative Judaism appears in what follows.

[V D] R. Zeirah in the name of R. Eleazar: "Were I to write for him my laws by ten thousands, they would be regarded as a strange thing" (Hos. 8:12). Now is the greater part of the Torah written down? [Surely not. The oral part is much greater.] But more abundant are the matters which are derived by exegesis from the written [Torah] than those derived by exegesis from the oral [Torah]."

[E] And is that so?

[F] But more cherished are those matters which rest upon the written [Torah] that those which rest upon the oral [Torah] . . .

[J] R. Haggai in the name of R. Samuel bar Nahman, "Some teachings were handed on orally, and some thing were handed on in writing, and we do not know which of them is the more precious. But on the basis of that which is written, "And the Lord said to Moses, Write these words; in accordance with these words I have made a covenant with you and with Israel" (Ex. 34:27), [we conclude] that the ones which are handed on orally are the more precious."

[K] R. Yohanan and R. Yudan b. R. Simeon – One said, "If you have kept what is preserved orally and also kept what is in writing, I shall make a covenant with you, and if not, I shall not make a covenant with you."

[L] The other said, "If you have kept what is preserved orally and you have kept what is preserved in writing, you shall receive a reward, and if not, you shall not receive a reward."

[M] [With reference to Deut. 9:10: "And on them was written according to all the words which the Lord spoke with you in the mount,"] said R. Joshua b. Levi, "He could have written, 'On them,' but wrote, 'And on them.' He could have written, 'All,' but wrote, 'According to all.' He could have written, 'Words,' but wrote 'The words.' [These then serve as three encompassing clauses, serving to include] Scripture, Mishnah, Talmud, laws, and lore. Even what an experienced student in the future is going to teach before his master already has been stated to Moses at Sinai."

[N] What is the Scriptural basis for this view?

[O] "There is no remembrance of former things, nor will there be any remembrance of later things yet to happen among those who come after" (Qoh. 1:11).

[P] If someone says, "See, this is a new thing," his fellow will answer him, saying to him, "this has been around before us for a long time."

Y. Hagigah 1:7

Here we have absolutely explicit evidence that people believed part of the Torah had been preserved not in writing but orally. Linking that part to the Mishnah remains a matter of implication. But it comes close to the surface when we are told that the Mishnah contains Torah-traditions revealed at Sinai. From there it requires only a small step to the allegation that the Mishnah is part of the Torah, the oral part.

To define the category of the Torah as a source of salvation, as does the Yerushalmi, we can point to a story that explicitly states that proposition. In this story we see that because people observed the rules of the Torah, they expected to be saved. If they did not observe, they accepted their punishment. So the Torah now stands for something more than revelation and life of study, and (it goes without saying) the sage now appears as a holy, not merely a learned, man. This is because his knowledge of the Torah has transformed him. Accordingly, we deal with a category of stories and sayings about the Torah entirely different from what has gone before.

> [II A] As to Levi ben Sisi: troops came to his town. He took a scroll of the Torah and went up to the roof and said, "Lord of the ages! If a single word of this scroll of the Torah has been nullified [in our town], let them come up against us, and if not, let them go their way."
>
> [B] Forthwith people went looking for the troops but did not find them [because they had gone their way].
>
> [C] A disciple of his did the same thing, and his hand withered, but the troops went their way.
>
> [D] A disciple of his disciple did the same thing. His hand did not wither, but they also did not go their way.
>
> [E] This illustrates the following apophthegm: You can't insult an idiot, and dead skin does not feel the scalpel.
>
> Y. Taanit 3:8

Here we see how taxa into which the word Torah previously fell have been absorbed and superseded in a new taxon.

The Torah is an object: "He took a scroll . . . " It also constitutes God's revelation to Israel: "If a single word . . . " The outcome of the revelation is to form an ongoing way of life, embodied in the sage himself: 'A disciple of his did the same thing . . . " The sage plays an intimate part in the supernatural event: "His hand withered . . . "

Can we categorize this story as a statement that the Torah constitutes a particular object or a source of divine revelation or a way of life? Yes and no. The Torah here stands not only for the things we already have catalogued, but it represents one more thing which takes in all the others. Torah is a source of salvation. How so? The Torah stands for or constitutes the way in which the people Israel saves itself from marauders. This straightforward sense of salvation will not have surprised the author of Deuteronomy.

In the canonical documents up to the Yerushalmi, we look in vain for sayings or stories that fall into such a category. True, we may take for granted that everyone always believed that, in general, Israel would be saved by obedience to the Torah. That claim would not have surprised any Israelite writers from the first prophets down through the final redactors of the Pentateuch in the time of Ezra and onward through the next seven hundred years. But, in the rabbinical corpus from the Mishnah forward, the specific and concrete assertion that by taking up the scroll of the Torah and standing on the roof of one's house, confronting God in heaven, a sage in particular could take action against the expected invasion – that kind of claim is not located, so far as I know, in any composition surveyed so far.

This stunningly new usage of Torah found in the Talmud of the Land of Israel emerges from a group of stories not readily classified in our established categories. All of these stories treat the word Torah (whether scroll, contents, or act of study) as source and gurantor of salvation. Accordingly, evoking the word Torah forms the center-piece of a theory of Israel's history and an account of the teleology of the entire system. Torah indeed has ceased to constitute a specific thing or even a category or classification when stories about studying the Torah yield not a judgment as to status (that is, praise for the learned man) but promise for supernatural blessing now and salvation in time to come.

To the rabbis the principal salvific deed was to "study Torah," by which they meant memorizing Torah-sayings by constant repetition and, as the Talmud itself amply testifies, profound analytic inquiry into the meaning of those sayings. The innovation is that this act of "study of Torah" imparts supernatural power of a material character. For example, by repeating words of Torah the sage could ward off the angel of death and accomplish other kinds of miracles as well. So Torah-formulas served as incantations. Mastery of Torah transformed the man engaged in Torah-learning into a supernatural figure who could do things ordinary folk could not do. The category of "Torah" had already vastly expanded so that through transformation of the Torah from a concrete thing to a symbol, a Torah-scroll could be compared to a man of Torah, namely, a rabbi. Once the principle had been established that salvation would come from keeping God's will in general, as Israelite holy men had insisted for so many centuries, it was a small step for rabbis to identify their particular corpus of learning, namely, the Mishnah and associated sayings, with God's will expressed in Scripture, the universally acknowledged medium of revelation.

The key to the first Talmud's theory of the Torah lies in its conception of the sage, to which that theory is subordinate. Once the sage reaches his full apotheosis as Torah incarnate, then and only then the Torah becomes a source of salvation in the present concrete formulation of the matter. That is why we traced the doctrine of the Torah in the salvific process through citation of stories about sages, living Torahs, who exercised the supernatural power of the Torah and served, like the Torah itself, to reveal God's will. Since the sage embodied the Torah and gave the Torah, the Torah came to stand for the principal source of Israel's salvation, not merely a scroll or a source of revelation.

The history of the symbolization of the Torah proceeds from its removal from the framework of material objects, even from the limitations of its own contents, to its transformation into something quite different and abstract, quite distinct from the document and its teachings. The Torah stands for this something more, specifically when it comes to be identified with a living person, the sage, and endowed with those particular traits that the sage claimed for himself. While we cannot say that the process of symbolization leading to the pure abstraction at hand moved in easy stages, we may still point to the stations that had to be passed in sequence. The word Torah reached the apologists for the Mishnah in its long-established meanings: Torah-scroll or contents of the Torah-scroll. But even in the Mishnah itself, these meanings provoked a secondary development – status of Torah as distinct from other (lower) status; hence Torah-teaching in contradistinction to scribal-teaching. With that small and simple step the Torah ceased to denote only a concrete and material thing – a scroll and its contents. It now connoted an abstract matter of status. Once made abstract, the symbol entered a secondary history beyond all limits imposed by the concrete object, including its specific teachings, the Torah-scroll.

— 9 —

The Dual Torah in Reprise: From the Mishnah through the Bavli

The history of the formation of Judaism is the story of how the crisis precipitated by the Mishnah was resolved by the Bavli. The path of Torah through the ages, marked by the first six centuries of the Common Era, is straight and true, harmonious and linear; it is the story of the impact of the appearance of a holy book beyond Scripture upon the lives and thought of the people who deemed that book to be authoritative.

The advent of the Mishnah around 200 demanded that people explain the status and authority of the new document. The lines of structure emanating from the Mishnah led to the formation of a vast and unprecedented literature of Judaism. The explosive force of the return to Zion, in the time of Ezra, had produced the formation of the Torah-book and much else. The extraordinary impact of the person and message of Jesus, among other things, had led to the creation of an unprecedented kind of writing in yet another sector of Israel's life. So too would be the case with the Mishnah, Israel's response to the disaster wrought by Bar Kokhba's calamity.

The reason the Mishnah, a philosophical essay rich in theoretical initiatives, which also served as a law code, presented a stunning challenge to its age and heirs, was its sponsorship in Israel's politics. To begin with, the Mishnah enjoyed the sponsorship of the autonomous ruler of the Jewish nation in the land of Israel, namely, Judah the Patriarch. The result was that the Mishnah served purposes other than simple learning and speculative thought.

Whatever had been intended for it, at its very beginnings the Mishnah was turned into an authoritative law code, the constitution, along with Scripture, of Israel in its land. Accordingly, when

101

completed, the Mishnah emerged from the schoolhouse and forthwith made its move into the politics, courts, and bureaus of the Jewish government of the land of Israel. Men (never women, until our own day) who mastered the Mishnah thereby qualified themselves as judges and administrators in the government of Judah the Patriarch as well as in the government of the Jewish community of Babylonia. As we know, over the next three hundred years, the Mishnah served as the foundation for the Talmuds' formation of the system of law and theology we now know as Judaism. Exegesis of the Mishnah furthermore defined the taxonomy for hermeneutics of Scripture.

The vast collection constituted by the Mishnah therefore demanded explanation. What is this book? How does it relate to the (written) Torah revealed to Moses at Mount Sinai? Under whose auspices, and by what authority, does the law of the Mishnah govern the life of Israel? These questions, we realize, bear political as well as theological implications. To begin with, the answers emerge out of an enterprise of exegesis, of literature. The reception of the Mishnah followed several distinct lines, each of them symbolized by a particular sort of book. Each book, in turn, offered its theory of the origin, character, and authority of the Mishnah. For the next three centuries these theories would occupy the attention of the best minds of Israel, the authorities of the two Talmuds, and the numerous other works of the age of the seed time of Judaism.

We now know full well the two lines of expansion and development – theological, therefore also literary. One line from the Mishnah stretched through the Tosefta – a supplement to the Mishnah – and the two Talmuds, one formed in the land of Israel, the other in Babylonia, both serving as exegesis and amplification of the Mishnah. The second line stretched from the Mishnah to compilations of biblical exegesis of three different sorts. First, there were exegetical collections framed partly in relation to the Mishnah and the Tosefta, in particular Sifra, on Leviticus, Sifre on Numbers, and Sifre on Deuteronomy. Second, exegetical collections were organized mainly in relation to Scripture, with special reference to Genesis Rabbah and Leviticus Rabbah. Third, exegetical collections focused on constructing abstract discourse out of diverse verses of Scripture but on a single theme or problem, represented by Pesikta de Rab Kahana.

This simple catalog of the types, range, and volume of creative writing over the three hundred years from the closure of the Mishnah indicates an obvious fact. The Mishnah stands at the beginning of a new and utterly original epoch in the formation of Judaism. Like such generative crises as the return to Zion for the nation as a whole and the advent of Jesus for his family and followers, the Mishnah ignited in Israel a great burst of energy. The extraordinary power of the Mishnah, moreover, is seen in its very lonely position in Israelite holy literature of its time and afterward. The subsequent literature, for centuries to come, would refer back to the Mishnah or stand in some clear-cut hermeneutical relationship to it. But for its part, the Mishnah referred to nothing prior to itself – except (and then, mostly implicitly and by indirection) to Scripture. So from the Mishnah back to the revelation of God to Moses at Sinai – in the view of the Mishnah – lies a vast desert. But from the Mishnah forward stretches a fertile plain.

The crisis precipitated by the Mishnah therefore stimulated wide-ranging speculation, inventive experiments of a literary and (in the nature of things) therefore also of a political, theological, and religious character. The Yerushalmi's work of defining and explaining the Mishnah in relation to the (written) Torah, interpreting the meaning of the Mishnah, expanding upon and applying its laws, ultimately precipitated the making, also, of compilations of exegeses of Scripture. The formation of the Talmuds and scriptural-exegetical collections thus made necessary – indeed, urgent – extraordinary and original reflection on the definition of the Torah, through inquiry into the nature of canon and scriptural authority, the range and possibilities of revelation. The results of that work all together would then define Judaism from that time to this. So the crisis presented opportunity, and Israel's sages took full advantage of the occasion.

What was this crisis? As far as Judaism was concerned, revelation had been contained in the Hebrew Scriptures, later on called the written Torah. True, God may have spoken in diverse ways. The last of the biblical books had been completed – as far as Jews then knew – many centuries before. How then could a new book claim status as holy and revealed by God? What validated the authority of the people who knew and applied that holy book to Israel's life? These questions defined the critical issue of formative Judaism from 200 to 600. The resolution of the problem defines Judaism today. Accordingly, the crisis precipitated by the Mishnah came about because of the urgent requirement of explaining what the Mishnah was in relation to the Torah of Moses; why the sages who claimed to interpret and apply the law of the Mishnah to the life of Israel had the authority to do so; and how Israel, in adhering to the rules of the Mishnah, kept the will of God and lived the holy life God wanted them to live.

Why should the Mishnah in particular have presented these critical problems of a social and theological order? After all, the Mishnah was hardly the first piece of new writing to confront Israel from the closure of Scripture to the end of the second century. Other books had found a capacious place in the canon of the groups of Israelites that received them and deemed them holy. The canon of some groups had made room for writings of apocryphal and pseudepigraphic provenance, so framed as to be deemed holy. The Essene library at Qumran encompassed a diverse group of writings, surely received as authoritative and holy, that other Jews did not know within their canon. So, as is clear, we have to stand back and ask why the Mishnah presented special and particularly stimulating problems. Why should the issue of the relation of the Mishnah to Scripture have proved so pressing in the circles of talmudic rabbis of the third, fourth, and fifth centuries? We have no evidence that the relation to the canon of Scripture of the Manual of Discipline, the Hymns, the War Scroll, or the Damascus Covenant perplexed the Teacher of Righteousness and the other holy priests of the Essene community. To the contrary, the Qumran documents appear side by side with the ones we know as canonical Scripture. The high probability is that, to the Essenes, the sectarian books were no less holy and authoritative than Leviticus, Deuteronomy, Nahum, Habakkuk, Isaiah, and the other books of the biblical canon that they, among all Israelites, revered.

The issue had to be raised because of the peculiar traits of the Mishnah itself. But the dilemma proved acute, not merely chronic, because of the particular purpose the Mishnah was meant to serve and because of the political sponsorship behind the document. As I have already indicated, the Mishnah provided Israel's constitution. It was promulgated by the patriarch – the ethnic ruler – of the Jewish nation in the land of Israel, Judah the Patriarch, who ruled with Roman support as the fully recognized Jewish authority in the Holy Land. So the Mishnah was public, not sectarian, not merely idle speculation of a handful of Galilean rabbinical philosophers, though in structure and content that is precisely what it was.

The Mishnah emerged as a political document. It demanded assent and conformity to its rules where they were relevant to the government and court system of the Jewish people in its land. The Mishnah therefore could not be ignored and had to be explained in universally accessible terms. Furthermore, the Mishnah demanded explanation not merely in relation to the established canon of Scripture and apology as the constitution of the Jew's government, the patriarchate of second-century land of Israel. The nature of Israelite life, lacking all capacity to distinguish as secular any detail of the common culture, made it natural to wonder about a deeper issue. Israel understood its collective life and the fate of each individual under the aspect of God's loving concern, as expressed in the Torah. Accordingly, laws issued to define what people were supposed to do could not stand by themselves; they had to receive the imprimatur of Heaven, that is, they had to be given the status of revelation. To make its way in Israelite life, the Mishnah as a constitution and code demanded for itself a theory of beginnings at (or in relation to) Sinai, with Moses, from God. As I pointed out above, other new writings had proved able to win credence as part of the Torah, hence as revealed by God and so enjoying legitimacy. But they did so in ways not taken by the Mishnah's framers. How did the Mishnah differ?

In the view of all of Israel until about 200 CE, God was understood to have revealed the divine word and will through the medium of writing. The Torah was a written book. People who claimed to receive further messages from God usually wrote them down. They had three choices in securing acceptance of their account. All three involved linking the new to the old. In claiming to hand on revelation they could: 1. sign their books with the names of biblical heroes, 2. imitate the style of biblical Hebrew, or 3. present an exegesis of existing written verses, validating their ideas by supplying prooftexts for them. From the closure of the Torah literature in the time of Ezra, around 450 BCE to the time of the Mishnah nearly seven hundred years later, we do not have a single book alleged to be holy and at the same time standing wholly out of relationship to the Holy Scriptures of ancient Israel. The pseudepigraphic writings fall into the first category, the Essene writings at Qumran into the second and third. We may point also to the Gospels, which take as a principal problem demonstrating how Jesus had fulfilled the prophetic promises of the Old Testament and, in other ways, had carried forward and even embodied Israel's Scripture.

Insofar as a piece of Jewish writing did not find a place in relationship to Scripture, its author laid no claim to present a holy book. The contrast between Jubilees and the Testaments of the Patriarchs, with their constant and close harping on biblical matters, and the several books of Maccabees, shows the differences. The former claim to present God's revealed truth, the latter, history. So a book was holy because in style, in authorship, or in (alleged) origin it continued Scripture, finding a place therefore (at least in the author's mind) within the canon, or because it provided an exposition on Scripture's meaning.

But the Mishnah made no such claim. It entirely ignored the style of biblical Hebrew, speaking in a quite different kind of Hebrew. It is silent on its authorship through sixty-two of the sixty-three tractates (the claims of Abot pose a special problem). In any event, nowhere does the Mishnah contain the claim that God had inspired the authors of the document. These are not given biblical names and certainly are not alleged to have been biblical saints. Most of the book's named authorities flourished within the same century as its anonymous arrangers and redactors, not in remote antiquity. Above all, the Mishnah contains scarcely a handful of exegeses of Scripture. These, where they occur, play a trivial and tangential role. Here is the problem of the Mishnah: different from Scripture in language and style, indifferent to the claim of authorship by a biblical hero or divine inspiration, stunningly aloof from allusion to verses of Scripture for nearly the whole of its discourse – yet authoritative for Israel.

So the Mishnah was not a statement of theory alone, telling only how things will be in the eschaton. Nor was it a wholly sectarian document, reporting the view of a group without standing or influence in the larger life of Israel. True, in some measure it bears both of these traits of eschatology and sectarian provenance. But the Mishnah was (and is) law for Israel. It entered the government and courts of the Jewish people, both in the motherland and also overseas, as the authoritative constitution of the courts of Judaism. The advent of the Mishnah therefore marked a turning point in the life of Israel. The document demanded explanation and apology.

The one thing one could not do, as a Jew in third-century Tiberias, Sepphoris, Caesarea, or Beth Shearim in Galilee, was ignore the thing. True, one might refer solely to ancient Scripture and tradition and live life within the inherted patterns of the familiar Israelite religion-culture. But as soon as one dealt with the Jewish government in charge of everyday life – went to court over the damages done to a crop by a neighbor's ox, for instance – one came up against a law in addition to the law of Scripture, a document the principles of which governed and settled all matters. So the Mishnah rapidly came to confront the life of Israel. The people who knew the Mishnah, the rabbis or sages, came to dominate that life. Their claim, in accord with the Mishnah, to exercise authority and the right to impose heavenly sanction came to perplex. Now the crisis is fully exposed.

The Mishnah therefore made necessary the formation of the Talmuds, its exegetical companions. Within the processes of exegesis of the Mishnah came the labor of collecting and arranging these exegeses, in correlation with the Mishnah, read line by line and paragraph by paragraph. The sorts of things the sages who framed the Talmuds did to the Mishnah, they then went and did to Scripture. Within the work of exegesis of Scripture was the correlative labor of organizing what had been said verse by verse, following the structure of a book of the Hebrew Bible. The type of discourse and the mode of organizing the literary result of discourse suitable for the one document served the other as well. The same people did both for the same reasons. So to the Tosefta, Sifra, and the Yerushalmi alike, the paramount issue was Scripture, not merely its authority but especially its sheer mass of information. The decisive importance of the advent of the Mishnah in precipitating the vast exegetical enterprise represented by the books at hand emerges from a simple fact: the documents all focus attention on the Mishnah in particular. Two of them, the Tosefta and the Yerushalmi, organize everything at hand around the redactional structure supplied by the Mishnah itself.

The importance of the Bavli's distinctive contribution now becomes entirely clear. The Bavli carried forward a long-established enterprise, namely, the forging of links between the Mishnah and Scripture. But the organizers and redactors of the materials compiled in the Bavli did something unprecedented. They allowed sustained passages of Scripture to serve, as much as sustained and not merely episodic passages of the Mishnah served, as main beams in the composition of structure and order. In a single document, the Mishnah and Scripture functioned together and for the first time in much the same way. The original thesis, that the Mishnah depended upon the written Torah and that all of its statements were linked to prooftexts of Scripture, now gave way to its natural and complete fulfilment. Once sets of verses of Scripture could be isolated and made to provide a focus of discourse, Scripture would join the Mishnah in a single statement, cut down and reshaped to conform to the model of the Mishnah.

So Scripture now joined the Mishnah in a new union, in mythic language, one whole Torah. In revising Scripture to recast it into that same discursive and rhetorical framework that defined how and where the Mishnah would serve, the authors – framers of larger-scale units of discourse, ultimate redactors alike – made their unique contribution. Imposing a literary and redactional unity upon documents so remarkably disparate in every respect as the Mishnah and Scripture, the Bavli's authors created something entirely their own but in no way original to them: Judaism in its final and complete statement, Judaism in conclusion. From this point forward, the Torah would expand and develop, but only by making its own and naturalizing within its realm initially-alien modes of thought and bodies of truth. Of these, two must be taken into account: philosophy in the Greco-Islamic tradition and mysticism. We now turn to ask how the Torah made these two important sources of religious truth its own.

10

The World-view of the Dual Torah and Philosophy: Maimonides and Judah Halevi

By the time of the Muslim conquest of the Middle East and North Africa in the seventh century, the Judaism of the dual Torah had fully defined its generative symbol, identified its critical question, and provided its self-evident answer. Furthermore, it had set forth the canonical literature that recapitulated the system as a whole. But if the way of life, world-view, and identification of its particular "Israel" as the social entity of the system possessed the power that I have attributed to it, only the succeeding ages would supply the proof. For a system takes shape at a single moment, confronting a specific circumstance.

If it endures – and time alone tells whether it is succeeding and remaining vital – then that same system must accommodate revisions and recapitulations of the initial crisis. It must also make provision within its supple and capacious structure for entirely fresh readings of the initial system. If it can do so, it can go forward, constantly defining those terms that, to begin with, the system admirably addresses. In the case of the Judaism of the dual Torah, that meant rehearsing here and there, now and again, the experience of exile and return in the peculiar formulation of the dual Torah that called for sanctification in the exile and salvation in the coming restoration. To remould in its own image and likeness whatever might happen and wherever it might take place, the system had to make a place for modes of thought and modalities of human experience scarcely imagined among its original framers.

That is precisely what has happened in the unfolding of the Judaism of the dual Torah from its formation, at the end of the seventh century, to our own day. The system endured in essentially the structure imparted to it by the framers of the Yerushalmi and its companion documents, in exactly the definitive formulation provided by the authorship of the Bavli, from the fourth century and the fifth century, into the nineteenth and twentieth centuries. And there is every indication that in two or three generations from now, this same Judaism will contine to thrive among that "Israel" that it has defined for itself, realizing in the everyday its way of life, shaping the imagination of entire societies with the imprint of its world-view, answering the always chronic but invariably critical and urgent questions it addressed at the start, in age succeeding age. So it was, so it is, so it will be: Judaism, pure and simple, if in rich variety and diversity.

How can we demonstrate the reason for the systemic endurance, indeed, for the remarkable power that sustained a tiny, weak, and pressured (and even, under certain catastrophic conditions, oppressed) group? The answer is by demonstrating how the system derived strength from change and renewed itself in the movement of time and circumstance. For that is precisely what happened.

To do this we take up three kinds of innovation: new modes of thought, new visions of the religious life with God, and new political circumstances. In each case we shall see the manner in which the great sages did more than merely accommodate change. They drew upon the new in the service of the enduring. In the encounter with philosophy, exemplified by Maimonides, they recast the modes of thought that defined the systems' world-view. In the meeting with mystical experience, exemplified by the Zohar and Hasidism, the sages of Judaism redefined the dimensions of the system's way of life, encompassing heaven and earth, heaven upon earth, in the intense meeting with God in the here and now. In the crisis of political change of profound consequence, represented by Reform Judaism, they reconsidered the character of "Israel," the holy people, and reframed the social metaphor represented by "Israel" in response to what they perceived to be a genuinely new and unprecedented political situation.

Let us begin with the philosophical challenge that yielded a new medium for the formation and expression of the world-view of the Judaism of the dual Torah. The rise of Islam from the seventh century onward brought important intellectual changes because of the character of Islamic culture. These changes impacted upon the dual Torah because Jews, who in the Near and Middle East had lived in Aramaic with Hebrew, not in Greek with Latin, now adopted Arabic as their language and the Arabic world-view, framed in response to Greco-Roman philosophy, as their culture. Specifically, Muslim theologians who could read Greek or who read Greek philosophy translated into Arabic developed a mode of thought along philosophical lines – rigorous, abstract, and scientific with special interest in a close reading of Aristotle. Jewish intellectuals, at least those of whom we are informed, followed suit. While in ancient times a school of Judaic philosophy in the Greek-speaking Jewish world, represented by Philo of Alexandria, read Scripture in the light of philsophical modes of thought, the sages of the Talmud did not follow in detail and with attention to philosophical doctrine that generalizing and speculative mode of thought.[1] They read Scripture within a different framework altogether.

As Judaic intellectuals within Islamic civilization faced the challenge of Muslim rationalism and philosophical rigor, they also read Scripture and the Oral Torah in a new way. The task was not simply to reconcile and accommodate the one with the other. Nor was the harmonization of competing doctrines at the heart of matters. The work for those engaged by philosophy and science (and not everybody was) was to naturalize, and treat as systemically native, modes of thought that were perceived as not only a challenge, but also the right way of thinking for all time. Just as today most Judaists cannot imagine denying the established truths of science while affirming the revelation of the Torah (no one thinks the world is flat, for instance, and the story of a seven-day-creation for geological and cosmological learning is set aside as well) so in medieval Islam no Judaic intellectuals could rest easy with the admission that Scripture and science, in its philosophical form, were not simply diverse media and expressions of a single, harmonious truth, that is, God's truth.

That is why, alongside study of Torah (spending one's life in

---

[1] As a matter of fact, the Mishnah is a profoundly philosophical book, using (some of) the methods of Aristotle to reach (some of) the doctrinal conclusions of neo-Platonism. But that is a very different phenomenon from the wholesale entry into the philosophical world characteristic of the great medieval intellectuals of Judaism. In my *Philosophy of Judaism: The Initial System* (in press) I have shown how the framers of the Mishnah naturalized philosophical media of thought for their own systemic purposes.

learning the Babylonian Talmud and later codes, commentaries, and rabbinical court decisions) a different sort of intellectual-religious life flourished in classical Judaism. It was the study of the tradition through the instruments of reason and the discipline of philosophy. For the whole history of the classical tradition, "study of Torah" predominated. The philosophical enterprise attracted small numbers of elitists and mainly served their specialized spiritual and intellectual needs. That does not mean the philsophical way was unimportant. Those who followed it included the thoughtful and the perplexed – those who took the statements of the tradition most seriously and, through questioning and reflection, intended to examine and then effect them. The philosophers, moreover, were not persons who limited their activities to study and teaching; they frequently occupied high posts within the Jewish community and served in the high society of politics, culture, and science outside the community as well. Though not numerous, the philosophers exercised considerable influence, particularly over the mind of an age that believed reason and learning, not wealth and worldly power, were what really mattered.

The philosophical way proved attractive only at specific times and under unique circumstances, while the received formulation of the Judaism of the dual Torah was always and everywhere characteristic. Philosophy proved uniquely important to Jews living in close contact with other cultures and traditions, like those of Hellenistic Alexandria in the first century of the Common Era, of ninth-century Muslim Baghdad, of Spain in the eleventh and twelfth centuries, of Christian Germany in the nineteenth century, and of twentieth-century America. In such settings, Jews not only coexisted in an open society with Gentiles – pagans, Muslims, Christians, Zoroastrians. They took seriously and respected the intellectual life of their neighbors and shared in their philosophy and science. They did not live isolated from or in ignorance of the dominant spiritual currents of the day. On the contrary, each particular group felt called upon to explain its chief ideas and doctrines in terms accessible to all others. Reason was conceived as the medium for such discourse.

Philosophy for Islam, Christianity, and Judaism flourished in a world of deep religious conviction, a conviction common to the several disparate communities. The issues of philosophy were set not by lack of belief, but by deep faith. Few, if any, denied providence, a personal God, and a holy book revealed by God through his chosen messenger. Everyone believed in reward and punishment, in a last judgment, and in a settling of accounts. The Jewish philosopher had to cope with problems imposed not only by the classical faith, but also by the anomalous situation of the Jews themselves. What was the meaning of the strange, unfortunate history of the Jews? How was philosophy to account reasonably for the homelessness of God's people, who were well aware that they lived as a minority among powerful, prosperous majorities – Christian or Muslim? If Torah were true, why did different revelations claiming to be based upon it flourish, while the people of Torah suffered? Why, indeed, ought one to remain a Jew when every day one was confronted by the success of the daughter religions? Conversion was always a possibility, an inviting one even under the best of circumstances, for a member of a despised minority.

For philosophy the easy answers (we are still being punished for our sins or we suffer now but our reward will be all the greater later on) were transparently self-serving. They proved unsatisfactory because they were too easy. Philosophy was, further, concerned with the eternal questions facing all religious people: Is God just? What is the nature of humanity? What is the meaning of revelation?

Where were answers to be found? The search was complicated by the formidable appeal of Greek philosophy to medieval Christian and Islamic civilization. Its rationalism, its openness, its search for pure knowledge challenged all revelations. Philosophy called into question all assertions of truth verifiable not through reason, but only through appeals to a source of truth not universally recognized. Reason thus stood, it seemed, against revelation. Mysterious divine plans came into conflict with allegations of the limitless capacity of human reason. Free inquiry might lead anywhere and so would not reliably lead to the synagogue, church, or mosque. And not merely traditional knowledge, but the specific propositions of faith and the assertions of a holy book had to be measured against the results of reason. Faith *or* reason – this seemed to be the choice.

For the Jews, moreover, the very substance of faith in a personal, highly anthropomorphic God, who exhibited traits of character not always in conformity with humanity's highest ideals and who in rabbinic hands looked much like the rabbi himself, posed a formidable obstacle. Classical conundrums of philosophy were further

enriched by the obvious contradictions between belief in free will
and belief in divine providence. Is God all-knowing? Then how can
people be held responsible for what they do? Is God perfect? Then
how can he change his mind or set aside his laws to forgive people?

No theologian in such a cosmopolitan, rational age could begin
with an assertion of a double truth or a private, relative one. The
notion that something could be true for one party and not for another,
or that faith and reason were equally valid and yet contradictory,
were ideas that had little appeal. The holy book had to retain the
upper hand: "Scripture as the word of God contained, of course,
absolute truth, while philosophy as a human activity could find its
truth only in reasoning."[2] The two philosophers we shall now
consider represent the best efforts of medieval Judaic civilization to
confront these perplexities.

The first is Moses Maimonides (1141–1205), who was at one and
the same time a distinguished student of the Talmud and of Jewish
law in the classical mode, a community authority, a great physician,
and a leading thinker of his day. His achievement was to synthesize
a neo-Platonic Aristotelianism with biblical revelation.[3] His *Guide to
the Perplexed*, published in 1190, was intended to reconcile the believer
to the philosopher and the philosopher to faith. For him philosophy
was not alien to religion but identical with it, for truth was, in the
end, the sole issue. Faith is a form of knowledge; philosophy is the
road to faith. His proof for the existence of God was Aristotelian. He
argued from creation to Creator, but accepted the eternity of the
world. Julius Guttmann describes his view as follows:

> Since, in addition to bodies which are both moving and moved,
> there are other bodies which are moved and yet are not causes of
> movement, there must also exist a being which moves without
> being moved. The second proof is based not on the movement of
> bodies but on their transition from potency to act: the transition

---

[2] Abraham S. Halkin, "The Judeo-Islamic Age," in Leo W. Schwarz, ed., *Great
Ages and Ideas of the Jewish People* (New York: Random House 1956), 245.

[3] Since that was precisely the philosophical character and position of the Mishnah,
it is no wonder that Maimonides was the first to write a sustained and systematic
commentary to the Mishnah, studied in its own terms and not as an occasion for
study of the Talmud. But his Mishnah commentary in no way seizes upon the
philosophical method or propositions of the Mishnah; it is mainly elucidatory.

presupposed the existence of an actualizing principle which is external to the being thus changed. The impossibility of an infinite regression of causes, just as it led in the first proof to prime mover, now serves to establish the existence of a first actualizing principle, free of all potentiality and hence also immaterial in nature . . . Maimonides can prove the origin of the world as a whole, from God, only by deduction from the contingent existence of things.[4]

God becomes, therefore, an "absolutely simple essence from which all positive definition is excluded."[5] One can say nothing about the attributes of God. He is purged of all sensuous elements. One can say only that God is God – nothing more – for God can only be *known* as the highest cause of being.

What then of revelation? Did God not say anything about himself? And if he did, what need for reasonings such as these? For Maimonides prophecy, like philosophy, depends upon the Active Intellect. But in the case of the prophets, "the Active Intellect impresses itself especially upon their imaginative faculty, which is why they express their teachings in a poetic or literary form, rather than in the ratiocinative form of the philosophers."[6] Prophecy is a gift bestowed by God upon humankind. The Torah and commandments are clearly important, but are not ultimately beyond question or reasonable inquiry. They, however, survive the inquiry unimpaired. The Torah fosters a sound mind and body:

All its precepts and teachings conspire to guide a man to the greatest benefits, moral and intellectual. Everything in the Torah, whether it be a law or a narrative or genealogy, is significant . . . intended to inculcate a moral or intellectual truth, to wean men away from wrong beliefs, harmful excesses, or dangerous indulgences. In its entirety, the Law is the supreme means whereby man realizes himself most fully.[7]

---

[4] Julius Guttmann, *Philosophies of Judaism: The History of Jewish Philosophy from Biblical Times to Franz Rosenzweig*. Translated by David Silverman (New York: Holt, Rinehart & Winston, 1964), 158.

[5] Ibid.

[6] Halkin, "Judeo-Islamic Age," 251.

[7] Ibid.

The greatest good, however, is not to study Torah in the sense described earlier, but to know God, that is, to worship and love him. Piety and knowledge of Torah serve merely to prepare people for this highest achievement. Study of Torah loses its character as an end in itself and is rendered into a means to a philosophical goal. This constituted the most striking transformation of the old values. Philosophical knowledge of physical and metaphysical truths "culminates in a purified conception of the nature of God. It is this kind of understanding that engenders the longing for God and the love of him."[8]

Maimonides provide a definition of Judaism. That definition comprised a list of articles of faith he thought obligatory on every faithful Jew: 1. existence of God, 2. his unity, 3. his incorporeality, 4. his eternity, 5. the obligation to worship him alone, 6. prophecy, 7. Moses as the greatest of the prophets, 8. the divine origin of Torah, 9. the eternal validity of Torah, 10. God's knowledge of man's deeds, 11. his righteousness and judgment, 12. his promise to send a Messiah, and 13. his promise to resurrect the dead. These philosophical principles were hotly debated and much criticized but, ironically, achieved a place in the life of Judaic piety. Although subjected to debate and criticism, in the end they were made into a hymn, *Yigdal*, which is always sung at the conclusion of synagogue prayer.

> 1. The living God we praise, exalt, adore
> He was, he is, he will be evermore.
> 2. No unity like unto his can be
> Eternal, inconceivable is he.
> 3. No form or shape has the incorporeal one
> Most holy he, past all comparison.
> 4. He was ere aught was made in heaven or earth
> But his existence has no date or birth.
> 5. Lord of the Universe is he proclaimed
> Teaching his power to all his hand has framed.
> 6. He gave his gift of prophecy to those
> In whom he gloried, whom he loved and chose.
> 7. No prophet ever yet has filled the place
> Of Moses, who beheld God face to face.

---

[8] Ibid.

8. Through him (the faithful in his house) the Lord
The law of truth to Israel did accord.
9. This Law of God will not alter, will not change
For any other through time's utmost range.
10. He knows and heeds the secret thoughts of man:
He saw the end of all ere aught began.
11. With love and grace doth he the righteous bless,
He metes out evil unto wickedness.
12. He at the last will his anointed send
Those to redeem who hope and wait the end.
13. God will the dead to life again restore.
Praised be his glorious name for evermore.[9]

The esoteric words of the philosopher were thus transformed into a message of faith, at once sufficiently complex to sustain critical inquiry according to the canons of the day and simple enough to bear the weight of the faith of ordinary folk and to be sung. The "God without attributes" is still guide, refuge, stronghold. It is a strange and paradoxical fate for the philosopher's teachings. Who would have supposed at the outset that the way of the philosopher would lead to the piety of the people?

Many, indeed, came to no such supposition. They found the philosophers presumptuous, inadequate, and incapable of investigating the truths of faith. But the critics of philosophy were themselves philosophers. The greatest was Judah Halevi (1080–1141), who produced *not* a work of sustained philosophical argument and analysis, but an imaginary set of dialogues between a king (the King of the Khazars, a kingdom which did, in fact, adopt Judaism several centuries earlier) in search of true religion and the advocates of the several religious and philosophical positions of the day, including Judaism. Judah Halevi, poet and mystic, objected to the indifference of philosophy to the comparative merits of the competing traditions. In philosophy's approach, "the ultimate objective is the knowledge of God. Religion is recommended because it inculcates the proper moral qualities in men, but no attention is paid to the question of

---

[9] Alice Lucas, translator, quoted in Bernard Martin, *Prayer in Judaism* (New York and London: Basic Books, 1968), 84–5.

which system of religious morality one ought to follow."[10] For the majority religions in the West – Islam and Christianity – such an indifference may have been tolerable, but *not* for a minority destined any day to have to die for the profession of faith.

Martyrdom will not be evoked by the unmoved mover, the God anyone may reach either through revelation or through reason. Only for the God of Israel will a Jew give up his or her life. By its nature, philosophy is insufficient for the religious quest: "It starts with assumptions and ends with mere theories."[11] It can hardly compete with – let alone challenge – the *history* of the Jewish people, a history recording extraordinary events starting with revelation. In invoking history and theology in criticism of science and philosophy, Judah Halevi represents the Talmud of the land of Israel, Genesis Rabbah and Leviticus Rabbah, and in the succession to the Mishnah, Avot and Tosefta. For, he asked, what has philosophy to do with Sinai, with the land, with prophecy? On the contrary the Jew, expounding religion to the king of the Khazars, begins not like the philosopher with a disquisition on divine attributes; nor like the Christian, who starts with the works of creation and expounds the Trinity; nor like the Moslem who acknowledges the unity and eternity of God. The Jew begins as follows (a passage found compelling by Judaists from then to now):

> I believe in the God of Abraham, Isaac, and Israel, who led the Israelites out of Egypt with signs and miracles; who fed them in the desert and gave them the Land, after having made them traverse the sea and the Jordan in a miraculous way; who sent Moses with His Torah and subsequently thousands of prophets, who confirmed His law by promises to those who observed and threats to the disobedient. We believe in what is contained in the Torah – a very large domain.[12]

The king then asks: Why did the Jew not say he believes in the creator of the world and in similar attributes common to all creeds?

---

[10] Halkin, "Judeo-Islamic Age," 253.

[11] Ibid.

[12] Cited from Isaak Heinemann, "Judah Halevi, Kuzari," in *Three Jewish Philosophers*, ed. by Isaak Heinemann, Alexander Altmann, and Hans Lewry (Philadelphia: Jewish Publication Society of America, 1960), 33.

The Jew responds that the evidence for Israel's faith is *Israel*, the people, this history and endurance, and not the kinds of reasonable truths offered by other traditions. The *proof* of revelation is the testimony of those who were *there* and wrote down what they heard, saw, and did. If so, the king wonders, what accounts for the despised condition of Israel today? The Jew compares Israel to the dry bones of Ezekiel:

> . . . these bones, which have retained a trace of vital power and have once been the seat of a heart, head, spirit, soul, and intellect, are better than bones formed of marble and plaster, endowed with heads, eyes, ears, and all limbs, in which there never dwelt the spirit of life.[13]

God's people is Israel; he rules them and keeps them in their present status:

> Israel amid the nations is like the heart amid the organs: it is the most sick and the most healthy of them all . . . The relationship of the Divine power to us is the same as that of the soul to the heart. For this reason it is said, *You only have I known among all the families of the earth, therefore I will punish you for all your iniquities* [Amos 3:2] . . . Now we are oppressed, while the whole world enjoys rest and prosperity. But the trials which meet us serve to purify our piety, cleanse us, and to remove all taint from us.[14]

The pitiful condition of Israel is, therefore, turned into the primary testimony and vindication of Israel's faith. That Israel suffers is the best assurance of divine concern. The suffering constitutes the certainty of coming redemption. In the end, the Jew parts from the king in order to undertake a journey to the land of Israel. There he seeks perfection with God:

> The invisible and spiritual *Shekhinah* [presence of God] is with every born Israelite of pure life, pure heart, and sincere devotion to the Lord of Israel. And the Land of Israel has a special relation to the Lord of Israel. Pure life can be perfectly lived only there.[15]

---

[13] Ibid., 72.
[14] Ibid., 75.
[15] Ibid.

The king objects to this. He thought the Jew loved freedom, but the Jew finds himself in bondage by imposing duties obligatory in residing in the land of Israel. The Jew replies that the freedom he seeks is from the service of men and the courting of their favor. He seeks the service of one whose favor is obtained with the smallest effort: "His service is freedom, and humility before him is true honor." He, therefore, turns to Jerusalem to seek the holy life. He closes his remarks:

> *Thou shalt arise and have mercy upon Zion; for it is time to favor her, the moment is come. For thy servants love her stones and pity her dust* [Psalm 102:14–15]. This means, Jerusalem can only be rebuilt when Israel yearns for it to such an extent that we sympathize even with its stones and its dust.[16]

Here we find no effort to identify Judaism with rational truth, but rather the claim that the life of the pious Jew stands above and indeed constitutes the best testimony to truth.

The source of truth is biblical revelation; it was public, complete, fully in the light of history. History, not philosophy, testifies to the truth and in the end constitutes its sole criterion. Philosophy claims reason can find the way to God. Halevi says only God can show the way to God, and he does so through revelation and therefore in history. For the philosopher, God is the object of knowledge.[17] For Halevi, God is the subject of knowledge: "The yearning heart seeks the God of Abraham; the labor of the intellect is directed towards the God of Aristotle."[18] And Israel has a specifically religious faculty which mediates the relationship to God, as we have seen in the references to the role of Israel among the nations as similar to the role of the heart among the limbs.

Halevi seeks to explain the supernatural status of Israel. The religious faculty is its peculiar inheritance and makes it the core of humanity. He thus "predicates . . . the supernatural religious faculty."[19] But while the rest of humanity is subject to the laws of nature, Israel is subject to supernatural, divine providence mani-

---

[16] Ibid., 126–9.
[17] Guttmann, *Philosophies*, 125.
[18] Ibid.
[19] Ibid., 126.

fested in reward and punishment. The very condition of the Jews, in that God punishes them, verifies the particular and specific place of Israel in the divine plan. The teaching of prophecy thus returns in Halevi's philosophy.

These two philosophers were part of a number of important thinkers who attempted to meet the challenge of philosophy and of reason by constructing a comprehensive theological system. But the uses of reason were not exhausted by the philosophical enterprise. Reason played a central role in the study of Torah. The settings, however, were vastly different. If in Judaic tradition salvation was never reduced to a "confession of a creed or theological agreement," still important efforts were made, such as the one of Maimonides, to produce just such a creed. It is not as is often asserted that Judaism had (or has) no theology. Such a statement is obviously absurd. It is simply that the theological idiom of the Judaic tradition often diverged from that of the Christian West. In Maimonides, we meet a theological mind quite capable of addressing itself to the issues confronting any religious tradition perplexed by philosophical reason. But Judah Halevi, so much more private, subjective, and particularistic, ends up in a suprarationalist position not far divorced from neo-Platonism.

Though similar to Muslim and Christian intellectuals in mentality, the Jewish philosophers had more in common with the talmudic rabbis than with gentile philosophers. The rabbis accepted the Bible and the Talmud as "the whole Torah," and so did the Jewish philosophers. Every important philosopher was also a rabbi, that is, in the sense of having achieved mastery of the sacred sciences. Both groups – rabbis who studied the Torah, meaning the Talmud and related writings, and philosophers who in addition to the Talmud studied nature and philosophy as part of the Torah of God at Sinai – devoted themselves to the articulation of the role of Torah in the life of Israel, to the meaning of the fate of Israel, and to the effort to form piety and shape faith. For both, *reason* was the means of reaching into Torah, of recovering and achieving truth. But truth is not only in the form of proposition. Religious truth comes from God through experience and encounter and even confrontation, and these are not always or even very often in the medium of words and ideas. The mystic, framing a way of life of Torah enriched by mystical experience with God, enlarged the dual Torah in yet another dimension.

11

The Way of Life of the Dual Torah and Mysticism: The Zohar, Hasidism

The Judaism of the dual Torah in ancient times and in the medieval and modern ages welcomed and placed a high value on mystical experience attained through prayer, asceticism, and devotion to godly service. God was and is a perpetual presence in the Judaic religious life: the "Thou" of the here and now and the everyday. The Judaism of the dual Torah furthermore made a place within Torah for holy books of mystical doctrine. In ancient times, it is clear, a mystical experience involving visions of God in the levels of the firmament was available to some sages. A continuing tradition of speculation about matters of mystical knowledge and experience flourished from late antiquity forward. That tradition came to its zenith in the most important work of mystical speculation and experience, the Zohar, a thirteenth-century work of immense proportions and commensurate influence. That document and those that flowed from it reshaped the way of life of the Judaism of the dual Torah, not only or mainly its world-view.

Indeed, so influential and ubiquitous was the influence of the Zohar and the mystic life it fostered that we may say simply, the Zohar, after the written Torah and the oral Torah, is the third component of the Judaism of the dual Torah. While we know that its author was Moses de Leon and that he wrote the Zohar in Spain between 1281 and 1286, we cannot be surprised that de Leon speaks in the name of important second-century rabbis. The mystics before and after the Zohar took for granted that their doctrines were Torah and derived from the same authorities who gave them Mishnah and other parts of the oral Torah. They further treated as fact the conception that their way of life and the way of life of the holy sages of the Talmud were identical. The intense inner life of direct encounter through prayer, doing of the commandments, and study of Torah thus strengthened the power of the rabbinic Torah-myth in the life of the Jewish people and, indeed, generated fructifying, creative forces in the way of Torah.

Especially important in the framing of the way of life was the conviction that every deed of a human being on earth has its counterpart in invisible reality in heaven. The talmudic stress on practical action elevated concrete deeds into the highest mode of religious expression. What a Jew did affected the profound reality. "Thus I do this *mitzvah* for the sake of the unity of the Holy One, blessed be He," was said by a mystic who was able to help effect the greater unity of the one God. The social effect was to lay stress on the performance of deeds that formed a pattern of religious living – deeds that the non-mystic performed habitually in a more mundane spirit and in an attitude of mere conformity. The mystic knew that one did things for a deeper, transcendent reason; the mystic therefore brought new devotion to the old, established way of life. He joined the community ever more concerned to do precisely what everyone else was doing anyhow, but for his own reason.

It is no accident that the greatest lawyers and Talmudists also were among the most profound and influential mystics. For example, the author of the code of Jewish law, Joseph Karo (*Shulhan Arukh*), believed that he received heavenly visitations from the Mishnah perceived as incarnate. A great biblical commentator, Nachmanides, introduced into his commentary on the Pentateuch important mystical considerations. The greatest genius of the talmudic tradition, Elijah, the Gaon of Vilna, who lived at the end of the eighteenth century, was a paragon of rabbinic rationality who also gave his best efforts to the study of the Zohar and other mystical writings. We cannot in fact locate a major legal authority who, after mystic literature became available, did not also devote himself in some measure to the study of mysticism.

The reason is that the law and the inner life of the believing Jew were understood to express one and the same pattern. The way of life was whole and harmonious. The former was the body and the latter the spirit; the former was the outer capsule and the latter the inner meaning. So when the mystics, for their part, undertook ascetic behavior, it was in the form of moral behavior. Ascetic renunciation led less to hair shirts and fasting – though there assuredly was self-torture – than to moral action, that is, giving up one's rights in favor of another. Because the Jewish mystic wanted to love God, he had also to love his neighbor.

This is how the practical expression of ascetic mysticism is described in a thirteenth-century book of mysticism, the *Book of the Pious*:

At all times you should love your Creator with all your heart and all your soul and take council with your heart and a lesson from man who is but worms; if a person give you ten gold pieces or more, how deeply engraved would his love be in your heart. And if he provides your support and the support of your children and of your household you would certainly think, "This man which I have never seen and who has extended to me such kindness I would not be able to repay for all the goodness he has shown me should I live a thousand years. I would love him with all my heart and with all my soul; he could not command me to do anything that I would not do for him, because both my wealth and my being are his." As with the love of man so with the love of the Holy One, blessed be He, raised and exalted be His fame. It is He who gives sustenance to all, how much better that we should cleave to the love of the Creator, fear Him, nor transgress His commands whether great or small. For we do not know the reward of each commandment, and the punishment for transgressions though they appear light in our eyes, as it is written, *When the iniquity of my supplanters compasseth me about* (Psalm 49:6). The transgressions to which a man becomes habituated in this world will encompass him in the Day of Judgement. If he is deserving his good deeds will bear witness for him. True and firm it is that we are not to transgress the commandments of our Creator, even one of the small ones, for a house full of gold and silver. If an individual says, "I will transgress a commandment and with the gold and silver they give me I will fulfill the difficult commandments. With this I will support the poor, invite wayfarers, I will do very many favors." These are the futile thoughts, for perhaps soon after the transgression he will die and not succeed to the gift. Moreover, if he should not die the money would soon be dissipated so that he dies in his sin. Come and see how much you should love your

Creator and who does wonderful kindnesses with you, He creates you from a decayed drop, He gives you a soul, draws you forth from the belly, then gives you a mouth with which to speak, a heart to understand, ears to hear the pure words of His mouth, which are refined as silver and pure gold. It is He who leads you on the face of earth, who gives sustenance to all, who causes death and gives life to all. In His hand are the souls of all the living. It is He who distributes your share of bread. What is there to say? For the mouth is unable to speak, the ear unable to hear, for to Him all praise is as silence, there is no end to the length of His days, His years will have no end, He is the King of kings, the Holy One, blessed be His name and His fame. It is He who has created the heavens and earth, sea, and all that is therein. He is the provider of all, for His eyes are open upon all men's paths recompensing each according to his ways and the fruit of his deeds, whether good or bad. Behold it is He who sets forth before men two paths, the path of life and the path of death, and says to you, *Choose life* (Deuteronomy 30:19). In spite of all this, we who are filled with worms do not think and do not set our hearts but to fill our appetites freely. We do not think that man's days are numbered, today he is here, tomorrow in the grave, that suddenly he dies. For no man rules over his spirit retaining it (forever). Therefore it is good for man to remove himself from all appetites and direct his heart to love and fear the Lord with all his heart at all times and revile the life of vanity. For we will not be able to humble ourselves and subdue our passion which thrusts us from the land of the living, except through subduing our heart and returning to our Maker in complete repentance, to serve Him and to do His will with a whole heart. Our sages have said, "Bread and salt shalt thou eat and water in measurement shall you drink and beware of gazing at women which drives a person from the world. Love humans and judge all people in the scale of merit." And this is what the Torah has said, *But in righteousness shalt thou judge thy neighbor* (Leviticus 19:15). Be humble before all, busy yourself with Torah, which is whole, pure and upright, and do not praise yourself for it, because for this were you created.[1]

---

[1] Scholom Alchanan Singer, trans., *Medieval Jewish Mysticism: The Book of the Pious* (Northbrook: Whitehall, 1971), 37–38.

The reason that, while mystic doctrine was important, the main impact of mysticism was upon the way of life of the dual Torah, is simple. Mysticism infuses the everyday with God's presence. Accordingly, the main purpose of mysticism for Judaism is that God is very real, and the desire of the mystic is "to feel and to enjoy Him; not only to obey but to approach Him." So says Abraham J. Heschel, the greatest theologian of Judaism in the twentieth century, who goes on: "They want to taste the whole wheat of spirit before it is ground by the millstones of reason. They would rather be overwhelmed by the symbols of the inconceivable than wield the definitions of the superficial."[2] What, then, is the mystic doctrine of God in Judaism? This is how Heschel answers that question:

Mystic intuition occurs at an outpost of the mind, dangerously detached from the main substance of the intellect. Operating as it were in no-man's land, its place is hard to name, its communications with critical thinking often difficult and uncertain and the accounts of its discoveries not easy to decode. In its main representatives, the cabbala teaches that man's life can be a rallying point of the forces that tend toward God, that this world is charged with His presence and every object is a cue to His qualities. To the cabbalist, God is not a concept, a generalization, but a most specific reality; his thinking about Him full of forceful directness. But He who is "the Soul of all souls" is "the mystery of all mysteries." While the cabbalists speak of God as if they commanded a view of the Beyond, and were in possession of knowledge about the inner life of God, they also assure us that all notions fail when applied to Him, that He is beyond the grasp of the human mind and inaccessible to meditation. He is the *En Sof*, the Infinite, "the most Hidden of all Hidden." While there is an abysmal distance between Him and the world, He is also called All. "For all things are in Him and he is in all things . . . He is both manifest and concealed. Manifest in order to uphold the all and concealed, for He is found nowhere. When He becomes manifest He projects nine brilliant lights that throw light in all

[2] Abraham Joshua Heschel, "The Mystical Elements of Judaism," in Louis Finkelstein, ed., *The Jews: Their History, Culture and Religion* (New York: Harper & Row, 1971), 284–5.

directions. So, too, does a lamp throw brilliance in all directions, but when we approach the brilliance we find there is nothing outside the lamp. So is the Holy ancient One, the Light of all Lights, the most Hidden of all Hidden. We can only find the light which He spreads and which appears and disappears. This light is called the Holy Name, and therefore All is One."

Thus, the "Most Recondite One Who is beyond cognition does reveal of Himself a tenuous and veiled brightness shining only along a narrow path which extends from Him. This is the brightness that irradiates all." The *En Sof* has granted us manifestations of His hidden life: He had descended to become the universe; He has revealed Himself to become the Lord of Israel. The ways in which the Infinite assumes the form of finite existence are called *Sefirot*. These are various aspects or forms of Divine action, spheres of Divine emanation. They are, as it were, the garments in which the Hidden God reveals Himself and acts in the universe, the channels through which His light is issued forth.[3]

Obviously, in so fresh and original a system, all the antecdent symbols and conceptions of Judaism are going to be revised and given new meanings. The single most striking revision is in the very definition of Torah. We know that for classical Judaism Torah means revelation, and revelation is contained in various documents – some of them written down and handed on from Sinai, others transmitted orally, also from Sinai. But for the mystic, Torah also becomes a "mystic reality." As Heschel explains:

The Torah is an inexhaustible esoteric reality. To enter into its deep, hidden strata is in itself a mystic goal. The Universe is an image of the Torah and the Torah is an image of God. For the Torah is "the Holy of Holies"; it consists entirely of the name of the Holy One, blessed be He. Every letter in it is bound up with that Name.

The Torah is the main source from which man can draw the secret wisdom and power of insight into the essence of things. "It is called Torah (lit.: showing) because it shows and reveals that which is hidden and unknown; and all life from above is comprised

---

[3] Ibid.

in it and issues from it." "The Torah contains all the deepest and
most recondite mysteries; all sublime doctrines both disclosed and
undisclosed; all essences both of the higher and the lower grades,
of this world and of the world to come are to be found there." The
source of wisdom is accessible to all, yet only few resort to it. "How
stupid are men that they take no pains to know the ways of the
Almighty by which the world is maintained. What prevents them?
Their stupidity, because they do not study the Torah; for if they
were to study the Torah they would know the ways of the Holy
One, blessed be He."

The Torah has a double significance: literal and symbolic.
Besides their plain, literal meaning, which is important, valid and
never to be overlooked, the verses of the Torah possess an esoteric
significance, "comprehensible only to the wise who are familiar
with the ways of the Torah." "Happy is Israel to whom was given
the sublime Torah, the Torah of truth. Perdition take anyone who
maintains that any narrative in the Torah comes merely to tell us
a piece of history and nothing more! If that were so, the Torah
would not be what it assuredly is, to wit, the supernal Law, the
Law of truth. Now if it is not dignified for a king of flesh and blood
to engage in common talk, much less to write it down, is it
conceivable that the most high King, the Holy One, blessed be
He, was short of sacred subjects with which to fill the Torah, so
that He had to collect such commonplace topics as the anecdotes
of Esau, and Hagar, Laban's talks to Jacob, the words of Balaam
and his ass, those of Balak, and of Zimri, and such-like, and make
of them a Torah? If so, why is it called the 'Law of Truth?' Why
do we read *The Law of the Lord is perfect . . . The testimony of the Lord
is sure . . . The Ordinances of the Lord are true . . . More to be desired are
they than gold, yea, than much fine gold* (Psalm 19:8–11). But assuredly
each word of the Torah signifies sublime things, so that this or
that narrative, besides its meaning in and for itself, throws light
on the all-encompassing Rule of the Torah."[4]

In Heschel's statement, we see how the long and influential
tradition of mysticism in Judaism was able to reinforce and vivify
rabbinic Judaism in its talmudic mode. It is clear that the mystic

[4] Ibid., 292–3.

finds in Torah meanings and dimensions not perceived in the earlier phases of talmudic Judaism. In many ways the mysterious power of the mystic is to see what lesser eyes cannot perceive. But the perception is there, and to the mystic and his audience it is very real. So Torah took on a richer meaning than it had had, even for the rabbi. Torah came to include both the literal meaning of the words and a deeper or symbolic meaning. It was made to yield the meanings not solely of its sentences, but now of each and every individual letter.

The essence of the mystic way is not contained within the notion of the deeper layers of meaning to be found within Torah. Rather, the essence of mysticism is the inquiry into the very essence of God. Mysticism became a powerful force in Judaism because the vivid encounter with God that it made possible was not present in any other mode of Judaism or Judaic religiosity. This is how Gershom C. Scholem explains the mystic encounter with God:

> The mystic strives to assure himself of the living presence of God, the God of the Bible, the God who is good, wise, just and merciful and the embodiment of all other positive attributes. But at the same time he is unwilling to renounce the idea of the hidden God who remains eternally unknowable in the depths of His own Self, or, to use the bold expression of the Kabbalists, "in the depths of his nothingness." This hidden God may be without specail attributes – the living God of whom the Revelation speaks, with whom all religion is concerned, must have attributes, which on another plane represent also the mystic's own scale of moral values: God is good, God is severe, God is merciful and just . . . The mystic does not even recoil before the inference that in a higher sense there is a root of evil even in God. The benevolence of God is to the mystic not simply the negation of evil, but a whole sphere of divine light, in which God manifests Himself under this particular aspect of benevolence to the contemplation of the Kabbalist.[5]

In many ways, then, mysticism must be seen as the ultimate, logical conclusion of that mode of Judaism which took shape in the

---

[5] Gershom C. Scholem, "Major Trends in Jewish Mysticism," in J. Neusner, ed., *Understanding Rabbinic Judaism* (New York: Ktav, 1978), 253–4.

aftermath of the messianic disasters of the first and second century.
For the encounter with God outside history and time – the direct
realization of the knowledge of God, who in some measure is hidden
and unknowable in the depths of his nothingness – removes the
mystic from the one thing that rabbinic Judaism proposed to
neutralize, namely, the vagaries of history. The essentially a-histori-
cal quality of mystical thinking accounts for the ready home provided
to mysticism by that form of Judaism which began with the Mishnah
and the Talmud and, we now see, came to fruition and fulfilment –
in the minds of many great talmudists – in the mystical realization
of the encounter with God's hidden self.

Philosophy was for the few. It did not last. Mystical experience
was for everybody, and it endured. Indeed, reshaping the Judaism
of the dual Torah and fulfilling its promise of the sanctification of
the everyday, it brought the foretaste of salvation: life with God. It
is no surprise, therefore, that from the Zohar onward, book after
book gave written form to the godly life and encounter of one
generation after another. Philosophy flourished mainly in Judaism
in the Islamic world, mysticism in the Judaism of both Christendom
and Islam. Philosophy characterized the life of Spain, southern
France, the Middle East, and North Africa. By mystics were everywhere. And, most telling, philosophy in its medieval form is dated;
it is read by scholars; it speaks to no one in its original language and
form. But mysticism today, on the eve of the twenty-first century,
renews itself day by day.

Long after the end of the philosophical movement, a mystical
Judaism within the dual Torah was formed that bridged the span
from medieval to modern times. Hasidism, a mystical movement
that took shape in the eighteenth century and came to fruition in
the nineteenth and twentieth, exemplifies the enduring power of
mysticism to inform the way of life of the dual Torah and so to
reinforce the observance and study of the Torah. That fact is
astonishing, given the fresh character of the doctrines of the movement on the one side, and the powerful opposition precipitated by it
on the other. The power of the original system of the dual Torah to
absorb diverse viewpoints and make them its own finds testimony in
the ultimate character of Hasidism.

The mystic circles in Poland and Lithuania in the eighteenth
century, within which Hasidism developed, carried on practices that

marked them as different from other Jews (for example, special
prayers, distinctive ways of observing certain religious duties, and
the like). First among the leaders of the movement of ecstatics and
anti-ascetics, Israel b. Eliezer Baal Shem Tov, "the Besht," worked
as a popular healer. From the 1730s onward he undertook travels
and attracted to himself circles of followers in Podolia, Poland,
Lithuania, and elsewhere. When he died in 1760, he left behind not
only disciples but a broad variety of followers and admirers in
southeastern Poland and Lithuania. Leadership of the movement
passed to a succession of holy men, about whom stories were told
and preserved. In the third generation, from the third quarter of the
eighteenth century into the first of the nineteenth, the movement
spread and took hold. Diverse leaders, called *zaddikim*, holy men and
charismatic figures, developed their own standing and doctrine.

Given the controversies that swirled about the movement, we
should expect that many of the basic ideas would have been new.
But that was hardly the case. The movement drew heavily on
available mystical books and doctrines, which from medieval times
onward had won a place within the faith as part of the Torah.
Emphasis on a given doctrine on the part of Hasidic thinkers should
not obscure the profound continuities between the modern movement
and its medieval sources. To take one example of how the movement
imparted its own imprint on an available idea, Menahem Mendel of
Lubavich notes that God's oneness – surely a given in all Judaisms
– means more than that God is unique. It means that God is all that
is: "There is no reality in created things. This is to say that in truth
all creatures are not in the category of something or a thing as we
see them with our eyes. For this is only from our point of view, since
we cannot perceive the divine vitality. But from the point of view of
the divine vitality which sustains us, we have no existence and we
are in the category of complete nothingness like the rays of the sun
in the sun itself . . . From which it follows that there is no other
existence whatsoever apart from his existence, blessed be he. This is
true unification . . . "[6] Since all things are in God, the suffering and
sorrow of the world cannot be said to exist. So to despair is to sin.

Hasidism laid great stress on joy and avoiding melancholy. Like

---

[6] Cited by Louis Jacobs, "Basic Ideas of Hasidism," *Encyclopaedia Judaica* 7:1404.

their earlier counterparts in the medieval Rhineland, the Hasidim of modern times further maintained that the right attitude must accompany the doing of religious deeds: the deed could only be elevated when carried out in a spirit of devotion. The doctrine of Hasidism further held that, "In all things there are 'holy sparks' waiting to be redeemed and rescued for sanctity through man using his appetites to serve God. The very taste of food is a pale reflection of the spiritual force which brings the food into being . . . "[7] Before carrying out a religious deed, then, the Hasidim would recite the formula, "For the sake of the unification of the Holy One, blessed be he, and his *Shekhinah* [presence in the world]." Because of this they were criticized. But the fundamental pattern of life, the received world-view contained in the holy canon of Judaism – these defined the issues. Hasidism therefore constituted a Judaism within Judaism – distinctive, yet in its major traits so closely related to the Judaism of the dual Torah as to be indistinguishable except in trivial details.

One of these details mattered a great deal, that is, the doctrine of *zaddikism*. The *zaddik*, or holy man, had the power to raise the prayers of the followers and to work miracles. He was the means through which grace reached the world, the one who controlled the universe through his prayers. The *zaddik* would bring humanity nearer to God and God closer to humanity. The Hasidim were well aware that this doctrine of the *zaddik* – the pure and elevated soul that could reach to that realm of heaven in which only mercy reigns – represented an innovation. So Jacobs:

> But if such powers were evidently denied to the great ones of the past, how does the *zaddik* come to have them? The rationale is contained in a parable attribute to the Maggid of Mezhirech . . . When a king is on his travels he will be prepared to enter the most humble dwelling if he can find rest there, but when the king is at home, he will refuse to leave his palace unless he is invited by a great lord who knows how to pay him full regal honors. In earlier generations only the greatest of Jews could attain to the holy spirit. Now that the *Shekhinah* [divine presence] is in exile, God is ready to dwell in every soul free from sin.[8]

---

[7] Jacobs, col. 1405.
[8] Jacobs, col. 1406.

The development of the doctrine of the *zaddik*, apparently an utter innovation, in fact carries forward a theme of the Zohar, a mystical document of the thirteenth century.

The principal figure of the latter, Simeon b. Yohai, an important rabbi in talmudic times, was seen by the Hasidim as the model for the veneration offered to the *zaddik*. In that way they linked themselves to the most ancient past, what to them was the Torah.[9] Nahman of Bratslav was identified with Simeon b. Yohai and held by his disciples to have formed the reincarnation of the talmudic authority. The conclusion drawn from that fact, Green points out, is not the one that would distinguish the *zaddik* and his followers from the rest of Judaism:

> Nahman was very cross with those who said that the main reason for the *zaddik*'s ability to attain such a high level of understanding was the nature of his soul. He said that this was not the case, but that everything depended first and foremost upon good deeds, struggle, and worship. He said explicitly that everyone in the world could reach even the highest rung, that everything depended upon human choice.[10]

While the *zaddik* was a superior figure, a doctrine such as that of Nahman brought the Hasidic movement into close touch with the rest of Jewry, with its stress on the equal responsibility of all Israel to carry on the work of good deeds and worship (not to mention study of the Torah). What was special, then, became the most appealing trait. So Green describes the legacy of Nahman of Bratslav, citing the record of the master's last great message:

> "Gevalt! Do not despair!" He went on in these words: "There is no such thing as despair at all!" He drew forth these words slowly and deliberately, saying, "There is no despair." He said the words with such strength and wondrous depth that he taught everyone, for all generations, that he should never despair, no matter what it is that he has to endure.

Green notes that the master had left "the example of a man who had

---

[9] Arthur Green, *Tormented Master. A Life of Rabbi Nahman of Bratslav* (Tuscaloosa: University of Alabama Press, 1979), 12.

[10] Ibid., 14.

suffered all the torments of hell in his lifetime, but had refused to give in to ultimate despair."[11] Rightly seeing this as emblematic of the matter at hand, we may also note how throughly in agreement would be the authorship of the Yerushalmi, Genesis Rabbah, and Leviticus Rabbah. Here we see the power of the Judaism of the dual Torah. It derived its renewed force from a restatement of the familiar in a fresh idiom and a reconsideration of the profane under the aspect of the holy.

By the 1830s the original force of the movement had run its course and the movement, beginning as a persecuted sect, now defined the way of life of the Jews in the Ukraine, Galicia, and central Poland, with offshoots in White Russia and Lithuania on the one side, and Hungary on the other. The waves of emigration from the 1880s onward carried the movement to the West and, in the aftermath of World War II, to the USA and the land of Israel as well. Today the movement forms a powerful component of Orthodox Judaism, and that fact is what is central to our interest. For by the end of the eighteenth century powerful opposition, led by the most influential figures of East European Judaism, characterized Hasidism as heretical. Its stress on ecstasy, visions, miracles of the leaders, its way of life of enthusiasm – these were seen as delusions, and the veneration of the *zaddik* was interpreted as worship of a human being. The stress on prayer to the denigration of study of the Torah likewise called into question the legitimacy of the movement. In the war against Hasidism the movement found itself anathematized, its books burned, its leaders vilified: "They must leave our communities with their wives and children . . . and they should not be given a night's lodging . . . it is forbidden to do business with them and to intermarry with them or to assist at their burial."[12]

Under these circumstances, the last thing anyone would anticipate would have been for Hasidism to find a place for itself within what would at some point be deemed Orthodoxy. But it did. For example, one of the most influential and important organizations within contemporary Orthodoxy, Agudat Israel, finds in Hasidim its principal membership. The acceptance of the movement came about through the development, within Hasidism, of centers of study of the

---

[11] Ibid., 265.
[12] Ibid.

Torah. The joining of Hasidic doctrine with the received tradition legitimated what had begun outside that tradition altogether (at least, outside in the view of those who deemed themselves insiders). The first Hasidic center of Torah-study came into being in the mid-nineteenth century, and by the end of that time the Lubavich sect of Hasidism had founded still more important centers. What began as a heretical movement within the span of a century had gained entry into the centers of the normative faith, and in another century had come to constitute the bulwark of that faith. I can imagine no greater testimony to the remarkable power and resilience of the Judaism of the dual Torah than the capacity of that system to make a place for so vigorous and original a movement as Hasidism.

— 12 —

The Definition of the "Israel" of the Dual Torah in an Age of Political Change: Reform Judaism

Reform Judaism, as a Judaism, began with modest changes in the liturgy but ended up the single most important and most effective Judaism of the nineteenth century in central Europe, and of the later twentieth century in America. The reason is that Reform Judaism forthrightly and articulately faced the political changes that redefined the conditions of Jews' lives and presented a Judaism closely tied to the inherited system of the dual Torah, fully responsive to those changes. Constructive and intellectually vital in its day, Reform Judaism said what it would do and did it. Still more interesting, because it was a movement that confronted the issues of the day and the Jews' condition, Reform Judaism found itself able to change itself, its own deepest concerns and values. Reform is the Judaism that shows us how the systemic component, "Israel," underwent revisions while remaining essentially what the Judaism of the dual Torah had said it was. That continuator-system made itself into an instrument for what Jews wanted and needed it to be, whatever that was. Consequently, in the matter of the system's social entity, Reform Judaism provides the model for the other Judaisms of its classification – continuators of the Judaism of the dual Torah – and furthermore set the issues for debate from then to our own day. No Judaism in the past two hundred years exercised deeper influence in defining the issues Jews would debate; none made a richer or more lasting contribution to the program of answers Jews within the realm of the dual Torah would find self-evident.

The single dominant concern of the framers of Reform Judaism derived from the Jews' position in the public polity of the several Christian, European countries in which they lived. From the perspec-

136

tive of the political changes taking place from the American and French Revolutions onward, the received system of the Judaism of the dual Torah answered the wrong questions. For the issue no longer found definition in the claims of regnant Christianity. A new question, emerging from forces not contained within Christianity, demanded attention from Jews affected by those forces. For those Jews, the fact of change derived its self-evidence from shifts in political circumstances. When the historians began to look for evidence of precedents for changing things, it was because their own circumstance had already persuaded them that change matters – change itself effects change. What they sought, then, was a picture of a world in which they might find a place, and it went without saying that that picture would include a portrait of a Judaic system – a way of life, a world-view, a definition of the Israel to live the one and believe the other.

The issue confronting the new Judaism derived not from Christianity, therefore, but from political change brought about by forces of secular nationalism, which conceived of society not as the expression of God's will for the social order under the rule of Christ and his church or his anointed king (emperor, Tsar), but of popular will for the social order under the government of the people and their elected representatives. This was a considerable shift. When society does not form the aggregate of distinct groups, each with its place and definition, language and religion, but rather undifferentiated citizens (male, white, wealthy, to be sure), then the Judaism that Jews in such a society have to work out also must account for difference of a different order altogether. That Judaism will have to frame a theory of "who is Israel" consonant with the social situation of Jews who will to be different, but not so different that they cannot also be citizens.

The original and enduring Judaic system of Reform correctly appeals to Moses Mendelssohn for its intellectual foundations, and Mendelssohn presented, in the words of Michael A. Meyer, an appeal "for a pluralistic society that offered full freedom of conscience to all those who accepted the postulates of natural religion: God, Providence, and a future life."[1] The protasis presents the important

---

[1] Michael A. Meyer, *The Origins of the Modern Jew. Jewish Identity and European Culture in Germany, 1749–1824* (Detroit: Wayne State University Press, 1967), 48.

component: a pluralistic society which, in the nature of things, constitutes a political category. Issues dominant from Mendelssohn's time forward concerned what was called "emancipation," meaning the provision for Jews of the rights of citizens. Reform theologians took the lead in the struggle for such rights. To them it was self-evident not only that Jews should have civil rights and civic equality, they should also want them. A Judaism that did not explain why the Jews should want and have full equality as part of a common humanity ignored the issues that preoccupied those who found, in Reform Judaism, a corpus of self-evident truths. To those truths, the method – the appeal to historical facts – formed a contingent and secondary consideration.

To understand the urgent character of the question of the social entity upon which Reform Judaism rested, we must recall the social foundations for the entire structure of the dual Torah. The Judaism of the dual Torah, in its inherited formulation, stood firm and unimpaired, if never for long intact and unchanged, from generation to generation. The reason is that the Christian West and the Islamic Near and Middle East and North Africa defined for its "Israel," that is, its social entity, precisely the compelling question that that Judaism had answered. But in the late eighteenth and nineteenth century, in the West, as the nation-state took shape and opened a secular space for politics, first in the USA and France, sweeping changes in the political circumstances in which Jews lived and the economic conditions in which they made their living produced urgent issues that formerly had drawn slight attention. Consequently, claims that had for so long demanded response competed with new issues altogether. Profound alterations in the definition of the system's social entity resulted.

These were of two kinds. Within the system, among Judaisms that appealed to its way of life and world-view, accepted the authority of its holy books, and deemed knowledge of the Torah the principal qualification of truth, the definition of the system's social entity, "Israel," changed within the framework of the dual Torah. Outside of the system, another system altogether, an essentially secular one, redefined not only "Israel" but the very character of the classifiction of "Israel." Among the many Judaic systems within the framework of the Judaism of the dual Torah, Reform Judaism proves most interesting. More than philosophy and as much as mysticism inclusive of Hasidism, Reform Judaism shows us the power of the initial question and the compelling force of its self-evidently valid answer.

The question – what are we to make of the condition of God's people when God has allowed Christendom, later Islam, with worldly success to speak in the name of Moses and of the Torah – now pressed with renewed force. For the very definition of what and who Israel is demanded a revision with consequent profound changes in the picture of the way of life that Israel was to follow. These changes of course appealed to the received world-view expressed in the canon, but the canon would be read in a different way from the prevailing one of history. The Judaism of the dual Torah continued in this Judaism, for its basic symbolic structure remained unimpaired; its holy books, and no others, retained paramount importance; its entire tradition continued to form the court of appeal and the source of justification. So the new came under the governance of the true which, to be sure, required the rewriting of history. After all, the Zohar had done matters no differently, and in imputing the methods, propositions, and rational values of Greco-Islamic philosophy to the Torah, Maimonides too had vastly reformed whatever he had in hand.

The redefinition of the social condition of the Jews, as that revision was coming to expression within the myth and forms of politics, accounted for the task at hand. The Jews had formerly constituted a distinct group, subordinated within a politics defined by appeal to the mythic structure and system of the kindred religious civilizations, Christian or Muslim. Now in the West they formed part of what was represented in the new and secular myth as an undifferentiated mass of citizens, all of them equal before the law, all of them subject to the same law. The Judaism of the dual Torah rested on the political premise that the Jews were governed by God's law and formed God's people. The two political premises – the one of the nation-state, the other of the Torah – scarcely permitted reconciliation.

Reform was not the only Judaism that addressed this new social situation, but it was the most interesting and important. All of the consequent Judaic systems in the nineteenth century – Reform Judaism, Orthodox Judaism, positive Historical Judaism (and, in the USA, Conservative Judaism) – each of them addressing issues regarded as acute and not merely chronic, alleged that they formed the natural next step in the unfolding of 'the tradition," meaning the

Judaic system of the dual Torah. Viewed from without, all of them did. For every one of them spoke of not only Scripture but also the Talmud and related writings; all of them therefore appealed to the myth of the dual Torah and its canon; all of them rightly called their authorities "rabbis," and above all, among themselves every one of them vigorously debated the agenda of issues defined by the dual Torah.[2]

Why insist, as I do, that Reform Judaism finds a comfortable place within the Judaism of the dual Torah? It is because of the persistent and urgent claim of the Reformers. In "Judaism" (meaning the Judaism of the dual Torah) Reform renews and recovers the true condition of the faith; it selects, out of a diverse past, that age and that moment at which the faith attained its perfect definition and embodiment. Not change but restoration and renewal of the true modes, the recovery of the way things were in that perfect, paradigmatic time, that age that formed the model for all time – these deeply mythic modes of appeal formed the justification for change, transforming mere modification of this and that into Reform.

From the time of Constantine to the nineteenth century, Jewry in Christendom had sustained itself as a recognized and ordinarily tolerated minority. The contradictory doctrines of Christianity – the Jews as Christ-killers to be punished, the Jews as witnesses to be kept alive and ultimately converted at the second coming of Christ – held together in an uneasy balance When the balance was upset, the Jews were wiped out or forced to leave their centuries-old homes.

---

[2] The view that from a later perspective the Judaisms of the nineteenth century look remarkably alike will have surprised their founders and framers. For they fought bitterly among themselves. But, I stress, the three Judaisms of continuity exhibit striking traits in common. All looked backward at the received system of the dual Torah. All sought justification in precedent out of a holy and paradigmatic past. All viewed the documents of that system as canonical, different of course on the relative merit of the several components. They concurred that texts to prove propositions deemed true should derive from those canonical writings (or from some of them). All took for granted the enduring, God-given authority of those writings. None doubted that God had revealed the (written) Torah at Sinai. All looked for validating precedent in the received canon. Differing on issues important to both world-view and way of life, all three Judaisms concurred on the importance of literacy in the received writings, on the lasting relevance of the symbolic system at hand, on the pertinence of the way of life (in some, if not in every detail), on the power of the received Judaism of the dual Torah to stand in judgment on whatever, later, would serve to continue that Judaism.

The pluralistic character of some societies (for instance, that of Spain) and the welcome accorded entrepreneurs in opening territories (for instance, Norman England, Poland, and Russia, White Russia and the Ukraine, in the early centuries of development) account still more than doctrine for the long-term survival of Jews in Christian Europe. The Jews, like many others, formed not only a tolerated religious minority but something akin to a guild, specializing in certain occupations: for example, crafts and commerce in the East. True, the centuries of essentially ordinary existence in the West ended with the Crusades, which forced Jewry to migrate to the eastern frontier of Europe. But until the twentieth century, the Jews formed one of the peoples permanently settled in Europe, first in the West, later in the East. It was only in modern times that the Jews as a whole found or even aspired to a position equivalent to that of the majority population in European societies.

Prior to that time the Jews found themselves subjected to legal restrictions regarding where they might live and how they might earn a living. They enjoyed political and social rights of a most limited character. In the East, where most Jews lived, they governed their own communities through their own administration and law. They spoke their own language, Yiddish. They wore distinctive clothing, ate only their own food, controlled their own sector of the larger economy, and ventured outside of it only seldom. In all, they formed a distinct and distinctive group. Commonly, the villages in which they lived found Jews and Christians living side by side, but in many of those villages Jews formed the majority of the population. These facts made for long-term stability and autonomy. In the West, the Jews formed only a tiny proportion of the population but, until modern times, lived equally segregated from the rest of the country beind the barriers of language, custom, and economic calling. So the Jews for a long time formed a caste, a distinct and clearly defined group, but within the hierarchy ordered by the castes of the society at hand.

A process called "emancipation," part of a larger movement of emancipation of serfs, women, slaves, Catholics (in Protestant countries, for instance, England and Ireland), and Protestants in Catholic ones (France, for example), encompassed the Jews as well. Benzion Dinur defines this process of emancipation as follows:

Jewish emancipation denotes the abolition of disabilities and inequities applied specially to Jews, the recognition of Jews as equal to other citizens, and the formal granting of the rights and duties of citizenship. Essentially the legal act of emancipation should have been simply the expression of the diminution of social hostility and psychological aversion toward Jews in the host nation . . . but the antipathy was not obliterated and constantly hampered the realization of equality even after it had been proclaimed by the state and included in the law.[3]

The political changes that fall into the process of the Jews' emancipation began in the eighteenth century and in half a century affected the long-term stability that had characterized the Jews' social and political life from Constantine onward. These political changes raised questions not previously found urgent and, it follows, also precipitated reflection on problems formerly neglected. The answers to the questions flowed logically and necessarily from the character of the questions themselves.

Clearly, in the nineteenth century, particularly in Western countries, a new order revised the political settlement covering the Jews, which had been in place for nearly the entire history of the West. From the time of Constantine forward, the Jews' essentially autonomous life as a protected minority had raised political questions that found answers of an essentially supernatural and theological character. Now the emancipation redefined those questions, asking about Jews not as a distinct group but Jews as part of some other polity altogether than the Jewish one. Those Jews who simply passed over retain no interest for us; Karl Marx, for example, converted to Christianity at an early age and produced no ideas important in the study of Judaism(s). But vast numbers of Jews in the West determined to remain Jewish and also to become something else. Their urgent question addressed the issue of how to be both Jewish and something else – a citizen of Germany or France or Britain. That issue would not confront the Jews of the Russian Empire until World War II and, together with the Jews of the Austro-Hungarian Empire, Rumania, and other Eastern European areas, these formed the vast majority of the whole.

---

[3] Benzion Dinur, "Emancipation," *Encyclopaedia Judaica* 6:696.

The Jews of the West, preoccupied with change in their political position, formed only a small minority of the Jews of the world – the Western frontier (extending to California in the farthest west of all) of the Jewish people. But their confrontation with political change proved paradigmatic. They were the ones to invent the Judaisms of the nineteenth century. Each of these Judaic systems exhibited three characteristic traits. First, each asked how one could be both Jewish and something else, that is, also a citizen or member of a nation. Second, each defined "Judaism" (that is, its system) as a religion, leaving ample space for that something else, namely, nationality, whether German (*Deutschtum und Judentum*, German-ness and Jewish-ness), British, French, or American. Third, each appealed to history to prove the continuity between its system and the received Judaism of the dual Torah. The resort to historical fact, the claim that the system formed the linear development of the past, the natural increment of the entire "history" of Israel, the Jewish people, from the beginning to the new day – that essentially factual claim masked a profound conviction concerning self-evidence. The urgent political question produced a self-evidently correct answer out of the history of politics constituted by historical narrative.

An appeal to history, particularly historical fact, characterized all three Judaisms. But, as usual, Reform Judaism proved intellectually the most rigorous and interesting. The Reformers stated explicitly that theirs would be a Judaism built on fact. The facts of history, in particular, would guide Jews to the definition of what was essential and what could be dropped. History then formed the court of appeal, but also the necessary link, the critical point of continuity. The Historical School took the same position, but reached different conclusions. History would show how change could be effected, and the principles of historical change would then govern. Orthodoxy met the issue in a different way, maintaining that "Judaism" was above history, not a historical fact at all. But the Orthodox position would also appeal most forcefully to the past in its claim that Orthodoxy constituted the natural and complete continuation of "Judaism" in its true form. The importance of history in the theological thought of the nineteenth-century Judaisms derives from the intellectual heritage of the age, with its stress on the nation-state as the definitive unit of society and on history as the mode of defining the culture and character of the nation-state.

History as an instrument of reform, further, had served the
Protestant Reformation, with its appeal to Scripture as against
tradition, its claim that it would restore Christianity to its historical
purity. Finally and most important, the supernaturalism of the
inherited Judaism of the dual Torah with its emphasis on God's
active intervention in history, on miracles, on a perpetual concern
for the natural implications of the supernatural will and covenant –
that supernaturalism contradicted the rationalism of the age. The
one thing Jewish thinkers wished to accomplish was to show the
rationalism, reason, and normality of the Judaisms they constructed.
Appealing to facts of history against the unbelievable claims of a
Scripture, they placed upon a positive and this-worldly foundation
that religious view of the world that, in the received system of the
dual Torah, rested upon a completely supernatural view of reality.

The three Judaisms of the age, which we see as continuous in
important ways, took as their task the demonstration of how they
formed out of the received and unwanted old Judaism something
new, different, and acceptable. For each that meant a recasting and
reshaping of materials that, as a matter of fact, no one really wished
to discard: the canonical books, the received symbols, the basic
structure of the way of life, the categories and issues of the world-
view of the dual Torah. The Judaisms of the nineteenth century were
born in the matrix of the received system of the dual Torah among
people who themselves grew up in a world in which *that* Judaism
defined what people meant by Judaism. That is why the questions
of analysis must address the fact that the framers of the Judaisms of
continuation could not evade the issue of continuity. They wished
both to continue and to innovate, and to justify innovation. That
desire affected Orthodoxy as much as Reform. In making changes,
they appealed to the past for justificatiion, but they pointed to those
changes also as proof that they had overcome an unwanted past. The
delicate balance between tradition and change attained by each of
the Judaisms of continuation marks the genius of its inventors. All
worked out the same equation: change but not too much, whatever
the proportion a group found excessive.

What made Reform the most interesting is that the Reformers
rejected important components of the Judaism of the dual Torah
and said so. Written Torah yes, oral Torah no, or maybe, or
sometimes. The Orthodox explicitly denied the validity of changing

anything, insisting on the facticity and the givenness of the whole. The Conservatives, in appealing to historical precedent, shifted the premise of justification entirely. Written Torah yes, oral Torah maybe. They sought what the Orthodox regarded as pointless and the Reform as inconsequential, namely, justification for making a few changes in the present in continuation of the processes that had effected development in the past. None of these points of important difference proved trivial. But all of them, together, should not obscure the powerful points of similarity that mark all three Judaisms as continuators of the Judaism of the dual Torah.

The three Judaisms were continuators, not lineal developments, not the natural next step, not the ineluctable increment of history, such as all claimed to be – each with good reason and, of course, all wrong. The points at which each Judaism took its leave from the received system do not match. In the case of Reform, the break proved explicit: change carried out by articulate, conscious decision, thus change as a matter of policy, enjoys full legitimacy.[4] As for the positive Historical School and its continuators in Conservative Judaism, the gulf between faith and fact took the measure of the difference between the received system of the dual Torah and the statement of mere historical facts that, for the Historical School, served to document the faith.

While the differences in the grounds of separation from the received system prove formidable, still more striking and fresh are the several arguments adduced to establish a firm connection to the Judaism of the dual Torah or, more accurately, to "the tradition" or to "Judaism." For the Judaisms of continuation characteristically differ in the several ways in which each, on its own, proposed to establish its continuity with a past perceived as discontinuous.[5] All three

---

[6] In Orthodoxy, the break came about by implication: the recognition of a distinct entity or religion, that is, Judaism as something distinct from the very ground of being, constituted a Protestant reading of religion, including Judaism. The capacity to treat as a component of life what the received tradition received as the ground of being marked the Orthodox as separate from the traditional. That premise as to the character of religion – something to be defined and known as formulated as faith and fact – vastly differed from the view of those to whom the received system of the dual Torah encompassed all of human existence.

[5] The Reform position proved least ambiguous: things change all the time, and we change things too. So Reform carries forward the method of the received Judaism. Stated differently, Reform simply pursues the precedent of all former Judaisms.

Judaisms enjoyed ample justification for the insistence, each in its way, that it carried forward the entire history of Judaism and took the necessary and ineluctible step beyond which matters had rested prior to its own formation. Reform in this regard found itself subjected to vigorous criticism, but in saying that "things have changed in the past and we can change them too," Reform established its primary position. It pointed to precedent and conceded the power of the received system to stand in judgment. All the more so did the Orthodox and Conservative theologians affirm that same power and place themselves under the judgment of the Judaism of the dual Torah.[6] In my view, all three established a firm position within the continuation of that Judaism. While the allegation of priority made

---

[6] Taking account of that same principle but expressing it in its distinctive way, the conservative theologians concurred that change is perennial and traditional. But they maintained two qualifications, one trivial, the other not. The minor qualification was that change must take place slowly and deliberately, on which point the Reform can readily have concurred. The major contribution laid emphasis on the possibility of identifying patterns of change, modes by which "the tradition" changed over time, the principles of change implicit in the history – the facts – of the "tradition." So, the Conservatives argued, change by itself falls outside all available modes of verification. We cannot know whether change out of the context of "the tradition" is right or wrong. But we can know that change within the lines already dictated by the history of the tradition is legitimate and right. How so? Change within the norms by which change has taken place marks the way forward, because that kind of change – which the Conservatives held, historical research tells the Conservatives how to define and effect – is legitimate. Indeed, change following from the natural pattern of the tradition represents nothing more than the natural next step of the tradition itself, and that claim constituted Conservative Judaism's most powerful apologetic. Conservative Judaism accepted change in principle, only with the proviso that the tradition dictate its own next step, and Conservative Judaism constitutes that natural next step. That theory of continuity with the tradition in no way compares to the one worked out by Reform Judaism. The Orthodox theory, of course, scarcely requires articulation: there is no change. How so? Everything Orthodoxy teaches simply states the doctrine, the way of life, the world-view, received from Sinai; all from God, through us. Yet the pattern of apologetics perceived in Conservative thought recurs: Orthodoxy too forms the natural next step. What is the sole point of difference between that position and the one of Conservative theologians? Orthodoxy perceived no difference between itself and "the tradition," while Conservative Judaism recognized the difference and constructed the required apologetic for it. So in the aspect of establishing continuity, Reform stood apart from the other groups, while the Orthodox and Conservative involed pretty much the same principle, though of course in different ways. The incremental theory of the linear history of Judaism, established within Orthodox and recapitulated by Conservative Judaism, of course would serve the Reformers as well, if playing a less central part in their theory of themselves.

by each, as the next step in the linear and incremental history of Judaism, scarcely demands serious analysis, the theory, for each one respectively, enjoys ample if not diverse justification.

When we focus upon Reform Judaism in particular, we locate a single dramatic moment at which the whole formation of a new Judaism within the dual Torah came to expression. That dramatic moment is in the statement that emerged from a meeting of Reform rabbis in Pittsburgh in 1885. At that meeting the American Reform rabbinate made a declaration of its definition of Reform Judaism. To the Reform rabbis in Pittsburgh, Christianity presented no urgent problems. The open society of America did. The self-evident definition of the social entity, Israel, therefore had to shift.

To understand the change in the definition of the systemic "Israel," we have to recall how the fourth-century rabbis balanced Israel against Rome, Jacob against Esau, the triumphant political messiah (seen as arrogant) against the Messiah of God, humble and sagacious. So Israel formed a supernatural entity and in due course would enter into that final era in God's division of time, in which Israel would reach its blessing. The supernatural entity, Israel, now formed no social presence. The Christian world, in which Christ ruled through popes and emperors, in which kings claimed divine right and the will of the church bore multiform consequences for society, and in which, by the way, Israel too was perceived in a supernatural framework (if a negative one) no longer existed. So the world at large no longer verified, as had the world of Christendom and Islam, that generative social category of Israel's life, *Israel as supernatural entity*. Then the problem of the definition of what sort of entity Israel did constitute and what sort of way of life should characterize that Israel, what sort of world-view should explain it – that problem produced a new set of urgent and ineluctable questions and, in the nature of things, also self-evidently true answers, such as we find in Pittsburgh.

Reform Judaism forthrightly and articulately faced the political changes that redefined the conditions of Jews' lives and presented a Judaism, closely tied to the inherited system of the dual Torah, fully responsive to those changes. For Reform Judaism in the nineteenth century the full and authoritative statement of the system – its world-view, with profound implications on its way of life, and its theory of who is Israel – came to expression not in Europe but in America, in a Pittsburgh assembly. At that meeting of the Central Conference of

American Rabbis, the Reform Judaism of the age, by now about a century in the becoming, took up the issues that divided the Judaisms and made an authoritative statement on them, one that most people could accept.

The very fact that the Judaism before us could conceive of a process of debate and formulation of a kind of creed tells us that this Judaism found urgent the specification of its systemic structure, testimony to a mature and self-aware frame of mind. We look in vain for equivalent convocations to set public policy, for example, in the antecedent thousand years of the Judaism of the dual Torah. Statements of the world-view, as these would emerge in diverse expressions of the received system, did not take the form of a rabbi's platform and did not come about through democratic debate on public issues. That world-view percolated upward and represented a rarely articulated and essentially inchoate consensus about how things really are and should be. The received system came to expression in how things were done, what people found needless to make articulate at all: the piety of a milieu, not the proposition of a theological gathering. That contrast tells us not merely that Reform Judaism represented a new Judaism but, of greater interest, that the methods and approaches of Reform Judaism enjoyed their own self-evident appropriateness. From that fact we learn how the qualities people found self-evidently right had changed over time.

In Pittsburgh in 1885 the American Reform rabbis issued a clear and accessible statement of their Judaism. We want to know one thing in particular about this Judaism, that is, its formulation of the issue of Israel as political circumstances defined it. Critical to the Judaism of the dual Torah was its view of Israel as God's people, a supernatural polity, living out its social existence under God's Torah. The way of life (sanctification) and the world-view (persistent reference to the Torah for rules of conduct and the explanation of conduct) began in the basic conception of who is Israel. Here too we find emphasis on who is Israel, with that doctrine exposing for all to see the foundations of the way of life and world-view that these rabbis had formed for the Israel they conceived. The platform stated:

We recognize in the Mosaic legislation a system of training the Jewish people for its mission during its national life in Palestine, and today we accept as binding only its moral laws and maintain only such ceremonies as elevate and sanctify our lives, but reject all such as are not adapted to the views and habits of modern civilization . . . We hold that all such Mosaic and rabbinical laws as regular diet, priestly purity, and dress originated in ages and under the influence of ideas entirely foreign to our present mental and spiritual state . . . Their observance in our days is apt rather to obstruct than to further modern spiritual elevation . . . We recognize in the modern era of universal culture of heart and intellect the approaching of the realization of Israel's great messianic hope for the establishment of the kingdom of truth, justice, and peace among all men. We consider ourselves no longer a nation but a religious community and therefore expect neither a return to Palestine nor a sacrificial worship under the sons of Aaron nor the restoration of any of the laws concerning the Jewish state . . .

I cannot imagine a more forthright address to the age. The Pittsburgh Platform takes up each component of the system in turn: Who is Israel? What is its way of life? How does it account for its existence as a distinct and distinctive group? Israel once was a nation ("during its national life") but today is not a nation. It once had a set of laws that regulate diet, clothing, and the like. These no longer apply because Israel now is not what it was then. Israel forms an integral part of Western civilization. The reason to persist as a distinctive group was that the group has its work to do, namely, to realize the messianic hope for the establishment of a kingdom of truth, justice, and peace. For that purpose Israel no longer constitutes a nation. It now forms a religious community.

What that means is that individual Jews do live as citizens in other nations. Difference is acceptable at the level of religion, not nationality, a position that accords fully with the definition of citizenship of the Western democracies. The world-view then lays heavy emphasis on an as-yet unrealized but coming perfect age. The way of life admits to no important traits that distinguish Jews from others since morality, in the nature of things, forms a universal category, applicable in the same way to everyone. The theory of Israel then forms the heart of matters, and what we learn is that Israel constitutes a "we," that is, that the Jews continue to form a group that, by its own indicators, holds together and constitutes a cogent social entity. It was, also, a truth declared, not discovered, and the self-evidence of the truth of the statements competed with the self-awareness characteristic of those who made them. They recognized the problem that demanded attention: the reframing of a theory of Israel for that Israel that they themselves constituted, the "we" that required explanation. No more urgent question faced the rabbis because they lived in a century of opening horizons in which people could envision perfection. World War I would change all that, also for Israel. By 1937 the Reform rabbis, meeting in Columbus, Ohio, would reframe the system, expressing a world-view quite different from that of the half-century before.

Among the Judaisms of the dual Torah, Reform Judaism ratified change now a generation old, proposed to cope with it, and so reframe and revise the received "tradition" as to mark out new limits for self-evident truth. For the nineteenth-century Jews of the West, the urgent problem was what Israel was in an age in which individual Jews had become something else in addition to being Israel. Is Israel a nation? No, Israel does not fall into the same category as the nations. Jews are multiple beings: Israel in one dimension, part of France or Germany or America in a second. But if Israel is not a nation, then what of the way of life that had made the nation different, and what of the world-view that had made sense of the way of life? These now formed the questions people could not avoid. The answers constituted Reform Judaism.

─── 13 ───

Beyond the Dual Torah:
Zionism

Zionism constituted the Jews' movement of self-emancipation, responding to the failure of the nations' promises of Jewish emancipation. It framed its world-view and way of life for the Israel of its definition in response to a political crisis, the failure, by the end of the nineteenth century, of promises of political improvement in the Jews' status and condition. Zionism called the Jews to emancipate themselves by facing the fact that gentiles in the main hated Jews. Founding a Jewish state where Jews could free themselves of anti-Semitism and build their own destiny, the Zionist system of Judaism declared as its world-view this simple proposition: the Jews form a people, one people, and should transform themselves into a political entity and build a Jewish state. Zionism stands wholly outside of the mythic framework and symbolic structure of the Judaism of the dual Torah. It identifies for itself the urgent question and the self-evidently valid answer that shapes the world-view and defines the way of life and, at the foundation of all things, defines the "Israel" of its system. It is the system that allows us to gain perspective on the Judaism of the dual Torah as separate, distinctive, and possessed of the linear and incremental history that I have now told in a brief way. Let me explain what is at stake in our inquiry into a Jewish system[1] different from one formed within the dual Torah.

My proposition that a short history of (a) Judaism, continuous and linear, derives from the formation and unfolding of the dual Torah, requires a test of falsification. For if I cannot show where my

---

[1] Not a Judaic system, for reasons explained in a moment.

thesis does not serve, I also cannot know that I am right about where
it does. It may be claimed that what I call (a) Judaism, that is, a
mythic structure and symbolic order, comprising a way of life, world-
view, and theory of the social entity that is (an) "Israel," is simply
"Judaism," pure and simple. So my claim that "Torah through the
ages" forms only one Judaism among a number, of times past and
our own day, requires a challenge. Can I point to a system comprising
world-view, way of life, and theory of "Israel" that stands totally
outside the symbol of Torah as defined within the myth of the dual
Torah? Can I appeal to the same theory of the history of Judaism to
account for the formation and success of that system distinct and
different from the Judaism of the dual Torah? Indeed, in Zionism I
can.

In the context of Reform Judaism with its powerful response to
the compelling question of who and what is the social entity that
forms the third element of the Judaism of the dual Torah, I can locate
another system that served very well. It is one that does not appeal
to the dual Torah. But in line with my original claim that all Judaisms
appeal to the Pentateuch, it is a system that calls upon the Pentateuch,
within the whole of the Hebrew Scriptures, as its foundation document. It is one that shapes a world-view in response to its theory of
who and what is Israel. That world-view is entirely incongruent with
the world-view of the Judaism of the dual Torah, deliberately and
systematically denying the claim of the canonical writings of the oral
Torah in appealing for the authority and program of its world-view.
It is one that utterly ignores the way of life of the Judaism of the dual
Torah. But it defines a way of life wholly harmonious with its world-
view. True, the system to which I refer cannot be classified as a
religion and, so far as we deem (a) Judaism to fall into the classification defined by religion in general, it is not a religion. But it is a
system that conforms to the requirements of any Judaism: world-
view, way of life, definition of the social entity, appealing to Scripture.[2]

---

[2] We need not be paralysed by the problem when a system is a religious system.
The ambiguity of Jews as an ethnic group that also forms, wholly in times past and
partially in our own day, a religious group, finds illustration in the case at hand,
which gives us not a Judaism in the sense in which a Judaism is a religion, but which
gives us a Jewish system in the sense in which the Jews form an ethnic group. The
ambiguity is simply an indicator of the contemporary social condition of the Jews
as a group, to which I referred earlier.

Zionism was founded in the World Zionist Organization, created in Basel in 1897. The urgent question identified by Zionism was the condition of the Jews in Europe, which Zionism defined as a political question. The self-evidently valid answer to the question was that, as a political entity, the Jews (or those Jews who wanted) should form a Jewish state. Accordingly, Zionism began with the consideration of the social entity, "Israel," of a system, and it defined the Jews as "a people, one people" who should have a state. So the social entity was now not supernatural but this-worldly and political in the same sense in which other "peoples" were political and should comprise nations. Half a century later, in 1947, the United Nations accepted that view and called for the creation of a Jewish state in Palestine (along with an Arab state in the same territory). In the process, of course, a world-view and a way of life took shape.

Zionism is one of two systems with an essentially ethnic but not religious character that were born within European Jewry on the eve of the twentieth century. The other system was Jewish Socialism-and-Yiddishism, which took shape in the Bund, a Jewish union organized in Poland in 1897. Both systems, to be called Jewish as ethnic rather than Judaic as religious, answered profoundly political questions. Their agenda attended to the status of the Jews as a group, the definition of the Jews in the context of larger political and social change. In the twentieth century powerful forces for social and economic change took political form in movements meant to shape government to the interests of particular classes or groups, the working classes or racial or ethnic entities, for instance. The Judaic systems of the century responded in kind. Zionism addressed the urgent question of anti-Semitism. Jewish Socialism presented a Judaic system congruent with the political task of economic reform through state action. The Jews would form unions and engage in mass activity of an economic and ultimately therefore of a political character.

Why did Zionism identify as urgent the political question formulated as "the Jewish problem"? At the end of the nineteenth century, the definition of citizenship, encompassing ethnic and genealogical traits, presented the Jews with the problem of how they were to find a place in a nation-state that understood itself in an exclusionary and exclusive, racist way – whether Nazi Germany or nationalist Poland or Hungary or Rumania or revanchist and irredentist France.

Zionism declared the Jews "a people, one people" and proposed as its purpose the creation of the Jewish State.

While the nineteenth-century Judaisms addressed issues particular to Jews, the matters of public policy of the twentieth-century Judaic systems concerned everyone, not only Jews. So both systems intersected with comparable systems – like in character, unlike in content – among other Europeans and Americans. Socialism then is the genus, Jewish Socialism the species. That fact meets the requirement set forth at the outset: a system that defined an "Israel," a world-view, a way of life, in response to an urgent question – but not a system that continued the dual Torah at all. Here we move from a set of Judaisms that form species of a single genus – the Judaism of the dual Torah – to a set of Jewish systems that have less in common among themselves than they do between themselves and systems wholly autonomous of Judaic world-views and ways of life. The reason is clear. The issues addressed by the two Jewish systems of the twentieth century, the crises that made those issues urgent, did not affect Jews alone or mainly. The crises in common derived from economic dislocation, which generated socialism, and also Jewish Socialism; and the reorganization of political entities, which formed the foundation of nationalism, and also Zionism. So as is clear, the point of origin of the nineteenth-century Judaisms locates perspectives from the dual Torah. Jews in the twentieth century, alas, had other things on their minds.

The systems of the twentieth century made no use of the intellectual resources of the Judaism of the dual Torah, even while extensively utilizing Scripture. Neither one of the systems regarded itself as answerable to the Judaism of the dual Torah. For the twentieth-century systems birth came about within another matrix altogether – the larger world of socialism and linguistic nationalism, for Jewish Socialism and Yiddishism; the realm of the nationalisms of the smaller peoples of Europe, rejecting the government of the international empires of Central and Eastern Europe, for Zionism. That explains why we do not uncover an incremental relationship between the Judaism of the dual Torah and its continuators on the one side, and Zionism and its companion, Jewish Socialism-and-Yiddishism, on the other.

Clearly, what had enjoyed the standing of self-evident truth for fifteen hundred years lost that standing and fell by the wayside in scarcely a hundred years thereafter. What made the difference? It was the abyss between the civilization of the West in its Christian form and that same civilization as it took new forms – secular and I think sinister forms. What pertinence did the Judaism formed in response to Christianity have, with its interest in Scripture, Messiah, and the long trends of history and salvation? The new world imposed its own categories: class and class struggle, the nation-state composed of homogeneous cultural and ethnic units – the lowest common denominator of bonding for a society, the search, among diverse and rootless people, for ethnic identity. These issues characterized a world that had cast loose the moorings that had long held things firm and whole.

The facts of Zionism are simple. Zionism came into existence at the end of the nineteenth century with the founding of the Zionist Organization in 1897, and reached its fulfilment and dissolution in its original form with the founding of the State of Israel in May 1948. Zionism began with the definition of its theory of Israel: a people, one people, in a secular sense. Then came the world-view, which composed of the diverse histories of Jews a single, singular history of the Jewish people (nation), leading from the land of Israel through exile back to the land of Israel. This component of the Zionist world-view constituted an exact recapitulation of the biblical narrative, even though it derived not from a religious but from a nationalist perspective.[3] This fact is illustrated by the statement of the greatest figure of Zionism in its history, David Ben-Gurion:

> I am not religious, nor were the majority of the early builders of modern Israel believers. Yet their passion for this land stemmed from the book of Books. That is why . . . though I reject theology, the single most important book in my life is the Bible.[4]

The way of life of the elitist or activist required participation in meetings, organizing within the local community, and attendance at national and international conferences – a focus of life's energy on the movement. Later, as settlement in the land itself became possible,

---

[3] As I have stressed, the persistent appeal to the Scriptures marks Zionism as fully withing the family of Judaisms even though, within contemporary categories, Zionism has to be called a Jewish, not a Judaic, system.

[4] Thomas R. Bransten, ed., *Recollections. David Ben-Gurion* (London: Macdonald Unit 75, 1970), 121.

Zionism defined as the most noble way of living life migration to the land and, for the Socialist wing of Zionism, building a collective community (kibbutz). So Zionism presented a complete and fully articulated Judaism and, in its day, prior to its complete success in the creation of the State of Israel in 1948,[5] one of the most powerful and effective of them all.

That in Zionism we deal with a response to an essentially political situation is self-evident. The word Zionism in modern times came into use in the 1890s with the sense of a political movement of "Jewish self-emancipation." The word "emancipation" had earlier stood for the Jews' receiving of political rights of citizens in various nations. This "self-emancipation" turned on its head the entire political program of nineteenth century Judaisms, as the obvious contrast with Reform shows us. That shift alerts us to the relationship between Zionism and the earlier political changes of which, at the start of the century, Reform Judaism had made so much. Two things had happened in the course of the nineteenth century to shift discourse from emancipation to self-emancipation: 1. disappointment with the persistence of anti-Semitism in the West, and 2. disheartening failures to attain political rights in the East.

Jews therefore began to conclude that they would have to attain emancipation on their own terms and through their own efforts. The stress on Zionism as a political movement, however, came specifically from Theodor Herzl, a Viennese journalist who, in response to the recrudescence of antisemitism he witnessed in covering the Dreyfus trial in Paris, discovered the Jewish problem and proposed its solution. To be sure, Herzl had earlier given thought to the problem of antisemitism, and the public antisemitism that accompanied the degradation of Dreyfus marked merely another stage in the development of his ideas. What Herzl contributed in the beginning was the notion that the Jews lived in a single situation, wherever they were located. They therefore should then live in a single country, in their own state, wherever it might be located. Antisemitism formed the antithesis of Zionism, and anti-Semites, growing in strength in European politics, would assist the Jews in building their state and thereby also solve their "Jewish problem."

---

[5] The Zionism of the post-1948 period faced a different set of issues not under discussion here.

The solution entailed the founding of a Jewish state, and that formed a wholly new conception, with its quite particular world-view and, in the nature of things, its rather concrete and detailed program for the conduct of the life of the Jews. For the Jews were now to become something they had not been for the "two thousand years" of which Zionism persistently spoke: a political entity. The Judaism of the dual Torah made no provision for a this-worldly politics, and no political tradition had sustained itself during the long period in which that Judaism had absorbed within itself and transformed all other views and modes of life. In founding the Zionist Organization in Basel in 1897, Herzl said that he had founded the Jewish state and that, in a half century, the world would know it, as indeed the world did.

Three main streams of theory flowed abundantly and side by side in the formative decades. One, represented by Ahad HaAm, laid stress on Zion as a spiritual center to unite all parts of the Jewish people. Ahad HaAm and his associates laid emphasis on spiritual preparation, ideological and cultural activities, and the long-term intellectual issues of persuading the Jews of the Zionist premises.[6] Another stream, the political one, maintained from the beginning that the Jews should provide for the emigration of the masses of their nation from Eastern Europe, then entering a protracted state of political disintegration and already long suffering from economic dislocation, to the land of Israel – or somewhere, anywhere. Herzl in particular placed the requirement for legal recognition of a Jewish state over the location of the state and, in doing so, he set forth the policy that the practical salvation of the Jews through political means would form the definition of Zionism. Herzl stressed that the Jewish state would come into existence in the forum of international politics.[7] The instruments of state – a political forum, a bank, a mode of national allegiance, a press, a central body and leader – came into being in the aftermath of the first Zionist congress in Basel. Herzl spent the rest of his life, less than a decade, seeking an international charter and recognition of the Jews' state.

A third stream derived from Socialism and expressed a Zionist

---

[6] S. Ettinger, "Hibbat Zion," in "Zionism," *Encylopaedia Judaica* 16:1031–1178.

[7] Arthur Hertzberg, "Ideological Evolution," in "Zionism," *Encylopaedia Judaica* 16:1044–1045.

vision of Socialism or a Socialist vision of Zionism. The Jewish state
was to be socialist, as indeed it was for its first three decades. Socialist
Zionism in its earlier theoretical formulation (before its near-total
bureaucratization) emphasized that a proletarian Zionism would
define the arena for the class struggle to be realized within the Jewish
people. The Socialist Zionists predominated in the settlement of the
land of Israel and controlled the political institutions for three
quarters of a century. They founded the labor unions, the large-scale
industries, the health institutions and organizations. They created
the press, the nascent army, the nation. No wonder that for the first
quarter-century after independence, the Socialist Zionists made all
the decisions and controlled everything.

The Zionism that functioned as a Judaism draws our attention to
the movement. In this regard Ahad HaAm made the explicit claim
that Zionism would *succeed* Judaism (meaning the Judaism of the
dual Torah). So Arthur Hertzberg states:

> The function that revealed religion had performed in talmudic
> and medieval Judaism, that of guaranteeing the survival of the
> Jews as a separate entity because of their belief in the divinely
> ordained importance of the Jewish religion and people, it was no
> longer performing and could not be expected to perform. The
> crucial task facing Jews in the modern era was to devise new
> structures to contain the separate individual of the Jews and to
> keep them loyal to their own tradition. This analysis of the situation
> implied . . . a view of Jewish history which Ahad HaAm produced
> as undoubted . . . that the Jews in all ages were essentially a nation
> and that all other factors profoundly important to the life of this
> people, even religion, were mainly instrumental values.[8]

Hertzberg contrasts that statement with one made a thousand years
earlier by Saadiah in the tenth century: "The Jewish people is a
people only for the sake of its Torah." That statement of the position
of the Judaism of the dual Torah contrasts with the one of Zionism
and allows us to set the one against the other, both belonging to the
single classification of "a Judaism." For, as is clear, each proposed
to answer the same type of questions, and the answers provided by

---

[8] Hertzberg, "Ideological Evolution," col. 1046.

each enjoyed that same status of not mere truth but fact, and not merely fact but just and right and appropriate fact.

As a Judaism entirely out of phase with the received system of the dual torah, Zionism enunciated a powerful doctrine of Israel. The Jews form a people, one people. Given the Jews' diversity, people could more easily concede the supernatural reading of Judaic existence than the national construction given to it. Scattered across the European countries as well as in the Moslem world, Jews did not speak a single language, follow a single way of life, or adhere in common to a single code of belief and behavior. What made them a people, one people, and further validated their claim and right to a state, a nation of their own, constituted the central theme of the Zionist world-view. No facts of perceived society validated that view. In no way, except for a common fate, did the Jews form a people, one people. True, in Judaic systems they commonly did. But the Judaic system of the dual Torah and its continuators imputed to Israel, the Jewish people, a supernatural status, a mission, a calling, a purpose. Zionism did not: a people, one people – that is all.

The world-view of Zionism came to expression in the form of historical narrative. For Zionist theory had the task of explaining how the Jews formed a people, one people, and in the study of "Jewish history," read as a single and unitary story, Zionist theory solved that problem. The Jews all came from some one place, traveled together, and were going back to that same one place – one people! Zionist theory therefore derived strength from the study of history, much as had Reform Judaism, and in time generated a great renaissance of Judaic studies as the scholarly community of the nascent Jewish state took up the task in hand. The sort of history that emerged took the form of factual and descriptive narrative. But its selection of facts, its recognition of problems requiring explanation, its choice of what mattered and what did not – all of these definitive questions found answers in the larger program of nationalist ideology. So the form was secular and descriptive, but the substance ideological in the extreme.

At the same time, Zionist theory explicitly rejected the precedent formed by that Torah, selecting as its history not the history of the faith, of the Torah, but the history of the nation, Israel construed as a secular entity. Zionism defined episodes as history, linear history, Jewish history, and appealed to those strung-together events, (all of a given classification to be sure) as vindication for its program of action. So we find a distinctive world-view that explains a very particular way of life and defines for itself that Israel to which it wishes to speak. True, like Reform Judaism, Zionism found the written component of the Torah more interesting than the oral. In its search for a usable past, it turned to documents formerly neglected or treated as not authoritative, for instance, the book of Maccabees. Zionism went in search of heroes unlike those of the present: warriors, political figures, and others who might provide a model for the movement's future and for the projected state beyond. So instead of rabbis or sages, Zionism chose figures such as David or Judah Maccabee or Samson. David the warrior king, Judah Maccabee, who had led the revolt against the Syrian Hellenists, Samson the powerful fighter – these provided the appropriate heroes for a Zionism that proposed to redefine Jewish consciousness, to turn storekeepers into soldiers, lawyers into farmers, corner grocers into builders and administrators of great institutions of state and government. The Judaism of the dual Torah treated David as a rabbi. The Zionist system of Judaism saw David as a hero in a more worldly sense – a courageous nation-builder.

Yet the principal components of Zionism's world-view fit entirely comfortably within the paradigm of the Torah of "Moses." For that Torah held, for its own reasons based on genealogy, that the Jews form a people, one people, and should (when worthy) have the land back and build a state on it. It is not surprising at all that Zionism found in the writings about the return to Zion ample precedent for its program, linking today's politics to something very like God's will for Israel, the Jewish people, in ancient times. So calling the new Jewish city Tel Aviv invoked the memory of Ezekiel's reference to a Tel Aviv, and that only symbolizes much else. Zionism would reconstitute the age of the return to Zion in the time of Ezra and Nehemiah, so carrying out the prophetic promises. The mode of thought, again, is entirely reminiscent of that of Reform Judaism which, to be sure, selected a different perfect world of mythic being, a golden age other than the one that glistened so brightly to Zionism.

The Zionist world-view explicitly competed with the religious one. The formidable statement of Jacob Klatzkin (1882–1948) provides the solid basis for comparison:

In the past there have been two criteria of Judaism: the criterion of religion, according to which Judaism is a system of positive and negative commandments, and the criterion of the spirit, which saw Judaism as a complex of ideas, like monotheism, messianism, absolute justice, etc. According to both these criteria, therefore, Judaism rests on a subjective basis, on the accceptance of a creed . . . a religious denomination . . . or a community of individuals who share in a *Weltanschauung* . . . In opposition to these two criteria, which make of Judaism a matter of creed, a third has now risen, the criterion of a consistent nationalism. According to it, Judaism rests on an objective basis: to be a Jew means the acceptance of neither a religious nor an ethnical creed. We are neither a denomination nor a school of thought, but members of one family, bearers of a common history . . . The national definition too requires an act of will. It defines our nationalism by two criteria: partnership in the past and the conscious desire to continue such partnership in the future. There are, therefore, two bases for Jewish nationalism – the compulsion of history and a will expressed in that history.[9]

Klatzkin's stress on "a will expressed in history" of course carries us back to the appeals of Reform and Conservative theologians to facts of history as precedents for faith. The historicism at hand falls into the same classification of thought. But for the theologians the facts proved episodic and *ad hoc*, mere precedents. Zionists would find it necessary to reread the whole of the histories of Jews and compose Jewish history of them, a single and linear system leading inexorably to the point which, to the Zionist historians, seemed inexorable: the formation of the Jewish state on the other end of time. Klatzkin defined being a Jew not as something subjective but something objective: "On land and language. These are the basic categories of national being."[10] That definition, of course, would lead directly to calling the Jewish state, "the State of Israel," so making a clear statement of the doctrine formed by Zionism of who is Israel.

In contributing, as Klatzkin said, "the territorial-political defi-

---

[9] Cited in Hertzberg, 317.
[10] Cited in Hertzberg, 318.

nition of Jewish nationalism," Zionism offered a genuinely fresh
world-view:

> Either the Jewish people shall redeem the land and thereby
> continue to live, even if the spiritual content of Judaism changes
> radically, or we shall remain in exile and rot away, even if the
> spiritual tradition continues to exist.[11]

It goes without saying that, like Christianity at its original encounter
with the task of making sense of history, so Zionism posited that a
new era began with its formation: "not only for the purpose of making
an end to the Diaspora but also in order to establish a new definition
of Jewish identity – a secular definition."[12]

In this way Zionism clearly stated the intention of providing a
world-view instead of that of the received Judaism of the dual Torah
and in competition with all efforts of the continuators of that Judaism.
So Klatzkin: "Zionism stands opposed to all this. Its real beginning
is *The Jewish State* [italics his], and its basic intention, whether
consciously or unconsciously, is to deny any conceptiion of Jewish
identity based on spiritual criteria." Obviously, Klatzkin's was not
the only voice. In his appeal to history, in his initiative in positing a
linear course of events of a single kind leading to one goal, the Jewish
state, Klatzkin did express that theory of history that would supply
Zionism with a principal plank in its platform. What the several
appeals to the facts of history would mean, of course, is that the arena
of scholarship as to what really happened would define the boundaries
for debate on matters of faith. Consequently the heightened and
intensified discourse of scholars would produce judgments not as to
secular facts but as to deeply held truths of faith, identifying not
correct or erroneous versions of things that happened but truth and
heresy, saints and sinners.

I have many times referred to the power of self-evidence, that is,
the capacity of a Judaism to identify the urgent question and to
respond with the self-evidently valid answer. We know that Zionism
has been the most influential and successful system of the twentieth
century, but that is not because of its success in creating the State of
Israel. It is because Zionism imposed its program upon the other

---

[11] Cited in Hertzberg, 319.
[12] Klatzkin, cited in Hertzberg, 319.

Judaisms with which it initially competed: Reform Judaism in mid-twentieth century became wholly Zionist, Conservative Judaism had been so from the start, and most of Orthodoxy concurred. The extraordinary success of this Judaism requires explanation. While the three continuators of the received system of the dual Torah worked out certain problems of conflict between doctrine and contemporary academic dogma, Zionism changed lives. No wonder, then, that it enjoyed the status of self-evident truth to the true believers of the movement which came in time to encompass nearly the whole of the contemorary Jewish world and to affect all the Judaisms of the day. It was, in other words, the single most successful Judaism since the formation fifteen hundred years earlier of the Judaism of the dual Torah.

The reason for the success of Zionism derives from that very source to which, to begin with, Zionism appealed: history, Jewish history. In a way no one would have wanted to imagine, what happened to Jews – Jewish history – validated the ideology of Zionism, its world-view, and furthermore vindicated its way of life. When the surviving Jews of Europe straggled out of the death camps in 1945, Zionism came forth with an explanation of what had happened and a program to effect salvation for the remnant. Critical to the self-evident truth accorded to Zionism is the historical moment at which Zionism came to realization in the creation of the Jewish state, the State of Israel.

Until the massacre of the Jews of Europe, between 1933 and 1945, and the founding of the State of Israel in 1948, Zionism remained very much a minority movement in Jewry. Jewish Socialism-and-Yiddishism in the new nations of Eastern Europe and the New Deal in American Democratic politics attracted a far larger part of Jewry, and the former, though not the latter, formed a competing Judaic system in particular. Before 1948 the Jewish population of the land of Israel/Palestine had scarcely reached half a million, a small portion of the Jews of the world. In the USA and in Western Europe Zionist sentiment did not predominate, even though a certain romantic appeal attached to the pioneers in the land. Until 1967 Zionism constituted one choice among many for Jews throughout the world. Since, at the present time, Jewry nearly unanimously attaches the status of the Jewish state to the State of Israel, affirms that the Jews form a people, one people, concedes all of the principal propositions of Zionism, and places the achievement of the Zionist program as the highest priority for Jewry throughout the world, we may say that today Zionism forms a system bearing self-evident truth for vast numbers of Jews.

Placing the state at the center of Judaic existence strikes vast numbers of Jews as self-evidently true, an obvious and ineluctable next step in the history of the Jews and, in that sense at least in the shared view of most of the Jews in the world, an inevitable increment in the history of Judaism as well. Zionism therefore inaugurated a long history for itself in a way in which its competing systems did not. Why did Zionism gain the support as a set of self-evident truths of the bulk of Jews in the world? Because Zionism, alone of the Judaisms of the nineteenth and twentieth centuries, possessed the potential of accurately assessing the power of antisemitism and its ultimate destiny. Zionism turns out to have selected the right problem and given the right solution (at least, so it now seems) to that problem.

The cheerful prognostications of world brotherhood, characteristic of Reform Judaism and of Socialism alike, perished, and the Reform Judaism of the nineteenth century lost its hold even on the heirs of the movement. But Zionism faced reality and explained it and offered a program, inclusive of a world-view and a way of life, that worked. The power of the Zionist theory of the Jews' existence came to expression not only at the end of World War II, when Zionism offered world Jewry the sole meaningful explanation of how to endure. It led at least some Zionists to realize as early as 1940 what Hitler's Germany was going to do. At a meeting in December, 1940, Berl Katznelson, an architect of Socialist Zionism in the Jewish community of Palestine before the creation of the State of Israel, announced that European Jewry was finished:

> The essence of Zionist awareness must be that what existed in Vienna will never return, what existed in Berlin will never return, nor in Prague, and what we had in Warsaw and Lodz is finished, and we must realize this! . . . Why don't we understand that is what Hitler has done, and this war is a kind of Rubicon, an outer limit, and what existed before will never exist again . . . And I declare that the fate of European Jewry is sealed . . .[13]

---

[13] Anita Shapira, *Berl: The Biography of a Socialist Zionist; Berl Katznelson* (New York: Cambridge University Press, 1985), 290.

Zionism, in the person of Katznelson, even before the systematic mass murder got underway, grasped that after World War II, Jews would not wish to return to Europe, certainly not to those places in which they had flourished for a thousand years. Zionism offered the alternative, the building of the Jewish state outside of Europe.

Anti-semitism in the early part of the twentieth century, yielding mass murder in the middle – these facts established a self-evidence of their own. The strength of Zionism lay in its confronting, at face value and in no subtle address, these very preponderant facts of Jewish existence as effectively and as persuasively as the Judaism of the dual Torah had taken up and sorted out the facts of Christian paramountcy through the fifteen hundred preceding centuries. That is why Zionism would dictate the setting in which other Judaisms of the edge would work out their systems, in one way or another. History proved Zionism right – history, not historians. Things that really happened made all the difference – actual events, not scholars' idle and self-indulgent speculation on the meanings and endings of events. In the full light of day Zionism presented self-evident truth. And, to conclude my argument in behalf of the proposition of this book, it was truth of a self-evidently different order from the truth of the Judaism of the dual Torah: discontinuous and not incremental, incongruent and not isomorphic, utterly without precedent and fresh. Zionism spoke to its Israel, providing obviously true answers to urgent and compelling questions. That is what marks it as a free-standing system, and it is also what shows the dual Torah too to be not merely Judaism but "*a* Judaism," among Judaisms, one that really does form a history, the history of Torah through the ages.

— 14 —

The Dual Torah in the History of Religion:
An Overview

Let us now consider the Judaism of the dual Torah from late antiquity
to modern times in the context of the history of religion. To begin with,
simple statement of fact suffices to summarize my characterization of
this history of (a) Judaism. As we have seen, the norm-setting
position of that Judaism was such that, until the nineteenth century,
all heresies within Judaism, schisms and fissures in the social
fabric, defined themselves against the system of the dual Torah.
All secondary expansions, revisions, developments, and modes of
renewal that came to expression adopted the mythic structure and
much of the canonical writings of that same Judaism. Consequently
the history of Judaism from late antiquity to modern times proves
cogent, since we can find a place for all later Judaic systems until the
late nineteenth century either within or in contrast to that one
Judaism and its system.

Within this picture, we may then identify the following periods in
the history of Judaism(s), in part reviewing what has been said in
foregoing sections. The histories of Judaisms are to be divided into
four periods: 1. the age of diversity, in which many Judaic systems
flourished, from the period of the formation of the Hebrew Scriptures
around 586 BCE to the destruction of the Second Temple in 70 CE; 2.
the formative age, from 70 CE to the closure of the Talmud of
Babylonia, around 600 CE; 3. the classical age, from late antiquity to
the nineteenth century, in which that original definition dominated
the lives of the Jewish people nearly everywhere they lived; and 4.
the modern age, from the nineteenth century to our own day, when
an essentially religious understanding of what it means to be Israel,

166

the Jewish people, came to compete among Jews with other views and other symbolic expressions of those views.

The Age of Diversity (586 BCE–70 CE)

In the first period there were various Judaisms, that is, diverse compositions of a world-view and a way of life that people believed represented God's will for Israel, the Jewish people. During that long age of nearly five hundred years, a number of different kinds of Judaism, that is, systems with a world-view and a way of life defining who is and who is not "Israel," or who is and who is not truly an heir to Scripture and its promises and blessings, came into being. During that time too the Judaism of the dual Torah came into being and competed for Jews' loyalty with those other Judaisms. We covered this age in chapters 2 and 3.

The Formative Age of Judaism (70–640 CE)

The formative period is to be divided into two parts, designated by the documents that preserve the systems that took shape in that time.

1. 70–200 CE. The first stage is represented by the Mishnah, a philosophical law code, around 200 CE in the consequence of the destruction of the Second Temple and the defeat of Bar Kokhba three generations later, emphasizing sanctification. The question addressed by the Mishnaic system was where and how Israel remained holy even without its holy city and temple.

2. 200–600 CE. The second stage is marked by the Talmud of the land of Israel, around 400 CE, also called the Yerushalmi or Jerusalem Talmud, an amplification and expansion of the Mishnah in the aftermath of the rise to political power of Christianity, presenting a dual emphasis on both sanctification and salvation. The question taken up by the Talmudic system – the dual Torah in its first definitive statement – was when and how holy Israel would be saved, even with a world in the hands of the sibling of Israel, Esau=Christendom, and later on in the power of the sibling, Ishmael=Islam, as well. A second Talmud, also serving to explain the Mishnah, took shape in Babylonia and reached closure around 600 CE. This other Talmud, called the Talmud of Babylonia or the Bavli, drew into itself a vast range of materials, treating both the Mishnah and Scripture, and presented the definitive statement of Judaism then to now.

The classical period of Judaism (640–1789)

A measure of the remarkable success of the Judaism of the dual
Torah is readily at hand. In 640, shortly after the closure of the
Talmud of Babylonia, when Islam swept across the Middle East and
North Africa which, by that point, had been Christian for half a
millennium, the Christian ocean evaporated as vast once-Christian
populations accepted Islam. Yet the small but deep pools of Judaisms
scarcely receded. That Judaic system that accounted for and made
tolerable Judaic subordination in the here and now explained this
new event. Christianity, however, which had triumphed by the sword
of Constantine, fell before the sword of Muhammad. On the other
hand, the same Judaic system flourished into the nineteenth century
in Eastern Europe and down to the middle of the twentieth century
for the great Judaic communities in Muslim countries, which is to
say, it remained the self-evident answer to the urgent question.

The Modern and Contemporary Scene (1789–)

In modern times, the diversity characteristic of the period of origins
has once again come to prevail. Now the symbolic system and
structure of the Judaism of the dual Torah has come to compete for
Jews' attention with other Judaic systems and with a widely diverse
range of symbols of other-than-Jewish origin and meaning.

This account of Judaism has presented a single field-theory
serviceable for the history of religion, a theory meant to deal with
the diversity of Judaic systems ("Judaisms") and to explain the
character of every Judaism that has emerged through time. The
same theory allows us to predict the shape of any Judaisms that will
come into existence in the future. This same approach can serve for
the study of Christianity, Islam, Buddhism, and other constructs
that hold together diverse data within the structure of an "ism."
That is how the history of the Judaism of the dual Torah may serve
as an example for our consideration of the other components of the
history of humankind's religions.

The reason is that this field-theory points to a particular selection
and interpretation of events of a distinctive sort. The character of
that selection then imposes its singular shape upon all systems – in
our case, Judaisms – that follow it, then to now. These events – loss
of the land, return to the land, which we remember are events that

are identified as important happenings, selected, but not experienced by any one person or generation or group – are understood to stand for exile, identified with everything people find wrong with their life, and return, marking what people hope will happen to set matters right. So each Judaism identifies what is wrong with the present and promises to make things tolerable now and perfect in the indeterminate future.

The inquiry into the generative paradigm and its definitive power may prove exemplary. How so? Any Judaism therefore stands for the identification by a social entity of a situation to escape, overcome, survive. Why does a Judaism succeed in perpetuating itself? Because the repeated pattern of finding the world out of kilter ("exile") *but* then making it possible to live for the interim in that sort of world, that generative paradigm perpetuates profound resentment. Why here? Why us? Why now? To the contrary, and this is the resentment, why not always, everywhere, and forever? So a Judaic religious system recapitulates a particular resentment. In this way each Judaism relates to other Judaisms and religious systems. Each one in its own way, on its own, will address and go over that same pattern, all addressing the same original experience. That is why a sequence of happenings, identified as important history and therefore paradigmatic event, is recapitulated in age succeeding age, whether by one Judaism in competition with another or by one Judaism after another. But, as a matter of systemic fact, no Judaism recapitulates any other, though each goes over the same paradigmatic experience.[1]

A further lesson we have learned for the study of a religion is to ask about the social entity to which and for which that religion speaks. If you agree that religion is public and social, then we start to study a religion by asking who holds that religion, where, when, and under what political circumstances. This emphasis upon the social world of religion leads us to want to know about the way in which a religion defines its social entity: the urgent questions facing that religious group, the self-evidently valid answers pertinent to its social and political circumstance.

---

[1] We remind ourselves that no Judaism stands in a linear relationship with any other, none forms an increment on a predecessor, and all constitute systems that, once in being, select for themselves an appropriate and useful past – that is, a canon of useful and authoritative texts. And that is the order: the system creates its canon.

When we identify Judaisms in one period after another, we begin by trying to locate, in the larger group of Jews, those social entities that see themselves and are seen by others as distinct and bounded, and that further present to themselves a clear account of who they are and what they do and why they do what they do: the rules and their explanations, their Judaism. This approach to the study of Judaism as a religion has rested on the simple premise that religion always is social and therefore also political, a matter of what people do together, not just what they believe in the privacy of their hearts.

No Judaic system can omit a clear picture of the meaning and sense of the category "Israel." Without an *Israel*, a social entity in fact and not only in doctrine, we have not a system but only a book. And a book is not a Judaism; it is only a book, except after the fact.[2] A Judaism for its part addresses a social group, an Israel, with the claim that that group is not merely an Israel but Israel, Israel *in nuce*, Israel in its ideal form, Israel's saving remnant, the State of Israel, the natural next step in the linear, continuous history ("progress") of Israel, everything, anything – but always Israel. So a Judaism or a Judaic system constitutes a clear and precise account of a social group, the way of life and world-view of a group of Jews, however defined.

A third lesson for the history of religions attends to diversity within a given religion or religious tradition. All religions encompass vast diversity and variety. If we pretend that Buddhism or Hinduism or Islam represent single, unitary, harmonious religions, all of them representing the outcome of a continuous tradition formed in an incremental history, we obscure the reality of Christianities, Islams, and Buddhisms. But how are we to deal with the differences within large and distinct families of religions: the varieties of Christianities,

---

[2] The importance of this principle of selection cannot be missed. Let me explain by way of example. I do not see the writings of Philo as a Judaism, though they may represent a Judaism. We have distinctive books that represent social groups, for instance, the apocalyptic writings of the Second Temple period, but our knowledge of those social groups – their way of life, their world-view, their identification of themselves as Israel – is imperfect. Consequently we cannot relate the contents of a system to its context or account for the substance of a system by appeal to its circumstance. We therefore know the answers provided by a system – that is, the contents of the book – but have not got a clear picture of the questions that the answers take up or, still more important, the political or social forces that made those questions urgent and inescapable in just that place in just that time.

Islams, Buddhisms, and Judaisms? Here we have had a case in point, in our working out the requirements of the theory that denies there is now or ever was a single Judaism.

True, there is no linear and incremental history of one continuous Judaism, beginning, middle, end, for there has never been Judaism, only Judaisms. But there is a single paradigmatic and definitive human experience, which each Judaism reworks in its own circumstance and context. In the case of all Judaisms, it is the experience of exile and return. In a broader sense, therefore, the present field-theory of the history of a particular religious tradition that comprises a variety of expressions may be summarized in the propositions that generalize on the case of Judaisms:

1. No religious system (within a given set of related religious systems) recapitulates any other (among that same set of closely related religious systems).

2. But all religious systems (within a given set) recapitulate resentment. A single persistent experience for generation after generation captures what, for a particular group, stands for the whole of the human condition: everything all at once, all together, the misery and the magnificence of life.

What we did for Judaism was to look into the Scripture common to them all and ask about the paradigm of human experience embedded in the deepest structure of that document. But that does not mean all Judaisms paraphrase one system. Recapitulating the story of the religion does not help us understand the religion. By contrast, identifying the point of origin of the story does. For the story tells not what happened on the occasion to which the story refers (the creation of the world, for instance) but how long afterward and for their own reasons people want to portray themselves. The tale therefore recapitulates that resentment, that obsessive and troubling point of origin, that the group wishes to explain, transcend, transform.[3]

Then how are diverse "versions" or, in my language, systems formed into one system? That is, how may we speak of not only

---

[3] Since all Christianities share the same books, the Torah, that for Judaisms portray the paradigmatic experience of exile and return, we have to wonder how the paradigm of resentment recapitulated makes its mark on the other family of biblical religious systems.

Judaisms but Judaism? The reason is that every Judaic system takes as urgent a set of questions deemed ineluctable and demanding answers. In one way or another the questions within a single and singular paradigm have persisted as the center of system after system. They turn on the identity of the group, they rest on the premise that the group's existence represents choice and not a given of nature or necessity. That obsessive self-awareness, a characteristic trait, masks a deeper experience that evidently defines for one generation after another and for one group of Jews after another that ineluctable question that collectively the group must answer. Why among the settled peoples of time the Jews, along with the Chinese and the Armenians among the oldest peoples of continuous historical existence on the face of the earth, should not have determined for themselves answers to the question of self-identification, is for us to find out.[4] To begin with, we recognize that the question is not a given, that other groups satisfactorily account for themselves and go on to other questions, and that the critical tension in the life of Jews' groups deriving from perplexity about the fundamental datum of group existence presents a surprise and a puzzle.

Let me spell out this theory, accounting for the character and definition of all of the diverse Judaisms that have taken shape since the destruction of the First Temple of Jerusalem in 586 and the return to Zion, building of the second Temple of Jerusalem, and writing down of the Torah, a process complete in 450 BCE. Since the formative pattern imposed that perpetual, self-conscious uncertainty, treating the life of the group as conditional and discontinuous, Jews have asked themselves who they are and invented Judaisms to answer that question. Accordingly, on account of the definitive paradigm affecting their group-life in various contexts, no circumstances have permitted Jews to take for granted their existence as a group.

Looking back on Scripture and its message, Jews have ordinarily treated as special what, in their view, other groups enjoyed as unconditional and simply given. Why the paradigm renewed itself is clear: this particular view of matters generated expectations that

---

[4] The Chinese do not obsessively ask, Who is a Chinese? And I have never heard an Armenian debate on the Armenian identity crisis, but – as we noted in chapters I and II – the government of the State of Israel faces collapse every time it tries to decide who is a Jew.

could not be met, hence created resentment – and then provided comfort and hope that made possible coping with that resentment. Promising what could not be delivered, then providing solace for the consequent disappointment, the system at hand precipitated in age succeeding age the very conditions necessary for its own replication.

It is therefore possible to classify all Judaisms as a single species of the genus religion, for all of them used some materials in common and exhibited some traits that distinguished all of them from other species of the genus religion, making of them a single species. Specifically each Judaism retells in its own way and with its distinctive emphases the tale of the Five Books of Moses, the story of a no-people that becomes a people, that has what it gets only on condition, and that can lose it all by virtue of its own sin. That is a terrifying, unsettling story for a social group to tell of itself, because it imposes acute self-consciousness, chronic insecurity, upon what should be the level plane and firm foundation of society. That is to say, the collection of diverse materials joined into a single tale on the occasion of the original exile and restoration because of the repetition in age succeeding age also precipitates the recapitulation of the interior experience of exile and restoration – always because of sin and atonement.

The power of all Judaisms to precipitate and then assuage resentment forms a useful point at which to conclude, because it forms a theory of the nature of religion that can be tested in the study of other religions, besides Judaism. That thesis about the nature of religion is as follows: religion recapitulates resentment. I mean two things, one psychological, the other political. In psychological terms, a generation that reaches the decision to change (or to accept or to recognize the legitimacy of change) expresses resentment of its immediate setting and therefore its past, its parents, as much as it proposes to commit itself to something better, the future it proposes to manufacture. In political change each Judaism addresses a political problem not taken up by any other and proposes to solve that problem. So when, in the second of the three theses, I say that the urgent question yields its self-evidently true answer, my meaning is this: resentment – whether at home or in the public polity – produces resolution. The two, when joined, form a religious system; in this context, a Judaism.

At issue when we study religion, therefore, is two things. First, we ask how in particular religious ideas relate to the political circumstances of the people who hold those ideas. Religion as a fact of the practical life of politics constitutes a principal force in the shaping of society and imagination alike, while politics for its part profoundly affects the conditions of religious beliefs and behavior. So one thing we should want to know when we study a religion, as we have seen in our study of Judaism(s), is how a stunning shift in the political circumstance of a religion affects that religion's thought about perennial questions.

But there is a second, more homely consideration. The one thing that the world at large does not always realize in contemplating the Jews is how much they enjoy being Jewish. Through most of the past, and today, they always have had, and now have, the choice: to be or not to be Jewish. (Only during the Judeocide carried out by the Germans between 1933 and 1945, when all Jews were condemned to death, was there no choice.) And, through the ages, nearly all Jews, nearly all the time, said yes to their origins and commitments. They wanted to be Jewish even though that meant being different from majorities wherever they lived outside of the Jewish state. They chose to be Jewish even though under Muslim, Christian, and secular governments that has meant to suffer discrimination. Were it not for a hundred generations of affirmation, the Jews would have perished, just as Abraham worried, right in the beginning: "After these things the word of the Lord came to Abram in a vision, 'Fear not, Abram, I am your shield; your reward shall be very great.' But Abram said, 'O Lord, God, what will you give me, for I continue childless, and the heir of my house is Eliezer of Damascus?' And Abram said, 'Behold, you have given me no offspring, and a slave born in my house shall be my heir'" (Gen. 15:1–3).

At the very beginning of Israel, the Jewish people, the patriarch Abraham worried for the future of the people, and, from then to now, Jews have thought of themselves, generation by generation, as possibly the last Jews on earth, "the ever-dying people," in the profound insight of Simon Rawidovicz. But the Jews survived, endured, triumphed – not the ever-dying people, but the ever-affirming people. And if you want to know the reason why, consider the Torah through the ages, because that is the reason why.

General Index

Abtalion, 22
Agriculture rules, 41, 43, 46–7
Ahad Ha'Am, 57–8
Alexander the Great, 31
Antigonos of Sokho, 21
Anti-Semitism, Zionism and Torah, 151–65
Aphrahat, 59
Appointed times, sabbath observance and festivals, 41–2, 44–5

Babylonian Talmud and formation of Judaism, 101–8
Banishment for crime, 47–8
Ben-Gurion, David, 19, 155
Book of the Hours, 124

Central Conference of American Rabbis, 147–8
Christianity, impact on development of Torah, 51–65
Chrysostom, John, 59
Civil and criminal law, 47–8
Cleanness and uncleanness, 46, 49
Commerce and trade, rules governing, 43
Conservative Judaism, 145–6; and Zionism, 161, 163
Constantine, Emperor, 55–8
Courts, role of and procedures, 47
Cyrus, King of Persia, 28, 32

Damages, rules concerning, 43, 46, 48
Death penalty for crime, 47
Dinur, Benzion, 141–2

Divorce and marriage, rules governing, 45–6
Dreyfus, Alfred, 156

Economic life of Israel, 38–50
Eleazar, and symbol of Torah, 95
Elijah, Gaon of Vilna, 123
Emancipation, Zionism and Torah, 151–65
Essenes and credence of Torah, 104–5
Eusebius, 59
Exile and return, Torah and Judaism, 25–37
Ezra and Pentateuchal Judaism, 25–37

Festivals and sabbath observances, 41–2, 44–5
Flogging for violations of law, 47–8

Gamaliel, 22
Gentiles, transactions with, 47
Green, Arthur, 133–4
Guide to the Perplexed, 114
Guttmann, Julius, 114–15

Haggai, and symbol of Torah, 96
Halevi, Judah, 109–21
Hama bar Uqba, 94
Haninah, teachings of scribes, 62
Hasidism, 139; Torah and way of life, 122–35; world-view of Torah, 110
Hertzberg, Arthur, 158
Herzl, Theodor, 156
Heschel, Abraham J., 126–8
Hillel, 22

175

Social reality: Pentateuchal
Judaism, 25–37; sanctification of
Israel, 38–50
State of Israel, Zionism and
Judaism, 151–65

Tanhum b. R. Hiyya, teachings of
scribes, 62
Temple cult, focus of Pentateuchal
Judaism, 25–37, 44, 48
Tithes and offerings, 43
Torah: in the age of diversity, 167;
authority in Babylonian Talmud,
76–87; dual Torah and formation
of Judaism, 101–8; in formation
of Judaism, 167; Judaism and
credence of Torah, 101–8; on the
modern and contemporary scene,
168–75; oral Torah as law code,
38–50; Palestinian Talmud and
sanctification, 51–65; rabbinic
authority in Babylonian Talmud,

76–87; status as symbol, 88–100;
temple rites as relationship to
God, 25–37; world-view, 109–21

Women, rights and property, 43,
45–6
World Zionist Organization, 152–3,
155, 175

Yiddishism and Judaism, 153
Yigdal, 116
Yohanan: symbol of Torah, 95–6;
teachings of scribes, 62
Yose b. Yoezer, 21
Yose b. Yohanan, 21
Yudan b. R. Simeon, symbol of
Torah, 96

Zachariah, 23
Zeira, 95
Zionism and Judaism, 151–65
Zohar, 8; Torah and way of life, 110,
122–35

Index of Biblical and Talmudic References